# Candide the Tenth
## and
## Other Agitations

# Candide the Tenth
## and
## Other Agitations

---

## PROSE AND POETRY

# MIKE SHARPE

Routledge
Taylor & Francis Group

LONDON AND NEW YORK

First published 2012 by M.E. Sharpe

Published 2015 by Routledge
2 Park Square, Milton Park, Abingdon, Oxon OX14 4RN
711 Third Avenue, New York, NY 10017, USA

*Routledge is an imprint of the Taylor & Francis Group, an informa business*

**Library of Congress Cataloging-in-Publication Data**

Sharpe, Mike
  Candide the tenth and other agitations : prose and poetry / by Mike Sharpe.
    p. cm.
  ISBN 978-0-7656-3677-5 (pbk. : alk. paper)
1. Current events—Literary collections. I. Title.

PS3619.H35665C36 2012
818'.609—dc23                                                    2012000737

ISBN 13: 9780765636775 (pbk)

To my wife, Carole,
and my children, Susanna, Matthew, Elisabeth, Hana
and in homage to my parents, Emma and Abraham

# Table of Contents

**Poetry**

**Selected Poems from *Thou Shalt Not Kill Unless Otherwise Instructed*, 2005**

# Preface

*Candide the Tenth* is a catalog of modern disasters witnessed by the contemporary descendant of Candide the First. The first Candide had a mentor named Pangloss who believed that we live in the best of all possible worlds. Voltaire showed that we do not live in the best of all possible worlds or even a reasonable facsimile. The tenth Candide has a mentor named Presto who believes that the world is far from the best possible but that we can do nothing about it. Both Candides question the hopeless views of their mentors. The difference between the eighteenth- and twentieth-first-century worlds is that those who lived in the older world could do little about the disasters while we can do a great deal. We have antibiotics. We have the know-how to provide food, drink, dwellings, care, and education for everyone. We can prevent war. We can even take stronger measures against natural disasters than our forebears could. Our problem is to find a way to use the available knowledge to extricate ourselves from the age-old habit of producing human debacles. The tenth Candide strives to learn how.

## Moral Injury

Recently the term moral injury has been coined to describe the affront to the soul suffered by men and women who go to war, kill, or witness killing, then come home and find that all they did and saw was a deep affront to their moral selves. Civilians also suffer from moral injury when they look at a world devastated by war and privation. The story "God Is Guilty" deals with our self-exculpating habit of attributing all the horrors that we commit to God's mysterious ways. "An End to Fighting" depicts the extreme consequences of moral injury. "Ruthless" dramatizes the difficulty of being good in a world in which survival depends on being bad. I would like to dodge this dilemma, but I pay taxes for wars that I do not believe in because I do not want to go to jail. I am 10 percent bad in spite of my desire to be 100 percent good.

## Backstage

Let me take you backstage for a moment. Often writers borrow from previous writers, with a clear conscience. I assume that Shakespeare among others had a clear conscience. I borrowed from *The Good Woman of Setzuan* by Bertolt Brecht to write "Ruthless." I borrowed from *New York Times* correspondent Elizabeth Rubin to write the battle scenes of "An End to War." She lived cheek by jowl for several months with an American platoon in the Korengal Valley of Afghanistan, and her article "Battle Company Out There" of February 24, 2008, is a vivid account of the fighting. I borrowed from the sociologist Erving Goffman, who wrote *The Presentation of Self in Everyday Life*, when I conceived "The Man of Many Masks." Goffman described how we present ourselves consciously or unconsciously in different ways depending on who we are and where we are. The wealthy present themselves differently in dress, manner, and speech than the poor. The educated present themselves differently than the uneducated. We all present ourselves differently to different audiences, attempting to adjust the impression that we make. We are in effect wearing a number of masks at different times and places. The wearing of masks creates the possibility of intentional deception as well as the possibility of detecting deception. No one plays this game with more ardor than a politician seeking to persuade the public that he is not playing this game.

The "Five Variations on Jack and Jill" are spoofs of five writers as well as five views of life. The letters to Emily Dickinson are homage to her and her sense of wonder at the strange universe in which we live, together with minor spoofing.

Some of my work has no precedents and sprang from my head with no human intervention. "The Day the World Came to an End" observes that we are victim or victimizer as a matter of chance. We could easily be one or the other. We are tied together by a common fate. "Do not ask for whom the bell tolls . . ." Perhaps there is a precedent for everything written.

## Moral Injury Again

I felt compelled to put the outcries of Cindy Sheehan, who lost her son in the Iraq war, and of Marie Fatayi-Williams, who lost her son in the London bombing of July 2005, into poetic form. They express the moral injury of victims with unbearable intensity.

## Quotes from Earlier Works

I have included several poems from *Thou Shalt Not Kill Unless Otherwise Instructed* and *Requiem for New Orleans*. *Thou Shalt Not Kill* was an immediate response to the Iraq war, but is also a response to any unnecessary war. *Requiem* was a response to the abandonment of New Orleans by the "political class," as it is called these days, but it is also a response to every abandonment by the political class and the class that pays them. I took the liberty of lifting the sequence called "Death" from *Requiem* and putting it in *Candide the Tenth* to express Candide's despair after leaving the ravaged city of New Orleans.

The four pieces from *Challenge*, an economics journal that I publish, are a mixed lot. "Little Red Riding Hood" and "JKG Versus the Angel" are fluff combined with a hint of economics. "The Truman Show" and "The Poorest Rich Country in the World: Address to the Graduating Class of 2011" are invitations to consider the possibilities and responsibilities that are ours for the taking. Come to think of it, this entire collection is such an invitation, with the few exceptions of fluff.

| November 24, 2011 |

# Acknowledgments

Thanks go to Angela Piliouras for her excellent job in supervising the production of this book, to Nancy Connick for flawless typesetting, to Susanna Sharpe for superb copy editing and proofreading, to Jesse Sanchez for his brilliant cover and interior design, to my family for sustaining me through the enjoyable time I had in writing this book, and to the many writers whose work I tried not to plagiarize.

# Candide the Tenth

and

## Other Agitations

# Candide the Tenth

# Chapter 1. My Background

I am the tenth-generation Candide. My great-grandfather nine generations back made a fortune in the slave trade. Each succeeding generation invested astutely in African gold mines, American plantations, German banking, and mercenary armies recruited from the Balkans. My father was the beneficiary of all this pecuniary activity and decided that a diversified portfolio of international investments suited his temperament best. The proceeds allowed him to live in a fifteen-thousand-square-foot mansion on a twenty-acre park in Greenwich and travel the world in his private jet when he was so inclined.

I was never close to him. My mother acted as intermediary. My father thought me excessively naïve, even after I went through Skull and Bones with the most sophisticated young men at Yale. After I graduated, he put me under the guidance of a tutor named Peter Presto, who happened to be an undercover agent for the CIA. I was not averse to traveling around the globe on a private jet to find out what my niche was in life, other than being the sole heir to a mansion and a fortune, since I have no sisters or brothers. In a nice but firm way, my father threw me out.

I am of medium build and tawny. The unofficial family history suggests some congress of the male line with Negresses and Jewesses, as they were called, and Russian, Turkish, and Chinese concubines over the last 250 years. That does not explain why I am of medium build. But it does explain why I am tawny.

Let me mention that I have been in love with the same girl since I was six years old. I cannot believe, no one can believe, that her name is Cunegonde. But it is true. I call her Connie. For some incomprehensible reason, her parents would not allow me to see her. We met surreptitiously until she grew up and became a physician and they no longer had any say in the matter.

Let me mention one more fact by way of introduction. I am by no means as ingenuous as was my progenitor ten generations back.

# Chapter 2. Tora Bora

My tutor Presto tells me his plan over a drink. He has obtained a press pass for me to accompany him wherever he goes. His current assignment takes us to Afghanistan. He is instructed to give a message to the commander of our Special Ops deployed in the foothills of the Tora Bora mountains. We fly to Kabul and then travel by helicopter to the foothills of the Tora Bora mountains on a cold, gray morning. I stand next to a grunt who happened to put down his M4 in order to open a Ready-to-Eat Meal. Out of curiosity, I picked up his rifle and casually looked into the distance through the gunsight. I was shocked to see a tall, bearded man dressed in local garb about five-hundred feet away. Bin Laden! I took careful aim, my finger was on the trigger, when the grunt grabbed his rifle from my hands.

"Haven't you heard? We've outsourced killing Bin Laden to the local tribal chief. Let's not spoil our relations with the locals. Didn't you know that Presto's mission here was to convey the decision of the Joint Chiefs to our commander?"

I didn't know. I trembled as I related all this to Presto. "The world has a way of taking its own course. We can't do anything about it."

# Chapter 3. I Meet Joe Wilson in Niger

Presto's next assignment was to meet Joe Wilson in Niger. Wilson was a State Department official who was sent to see if anybody was selling yellowcake to Saddam Hussein. I went along on the strength of my press credentials.

I learned that yellowcake is a crusty material that can be processed into uranium to make fissionable material for power plants or bombs. It's stored in aluminum tubes.

We arrived in the sand-blown, grimy capital, Niamey, at dusk and stayed overnight at a fleabag hotel.

In the morning Presto hooked up with Joe Wilson, who had an appointment with Niger government officials and European businessmen who operated the two uranium mines, both owned by the French. I tagged along.

A typical conversation went this way:

Wilson: "The U.S. government has information that Niger is shipping yellowcake to Iraq."

Nigerien president: "We have looked everywhere and find no evidence of such shipments. The controls on shipments are airtight."

Same question to U.S. ambassador. Same answer.

Same question to European operators of mines. Same answer.

Since I'm supposed to be a correspondent, I took notes on the meetings.

We hitched a ride back to Washington on an Army C-17. Joe Wilson filed his report, which was not what the administration wanted to hear. So they attacked him as incompetent. For good measure, they outed his wife, who was an undercover CIA operative.

I was amazed. Colin Powell presented a forged document to the UN purporting to show that Iraq was trying to buy aluminum tubes of yellowcake from Niger. The forged document came from the British who got it from the Italians who got it from a mysterious lady who worked for the Niger embassy in Rome, and then we attacked Iraq.

I remonstrated with Presto. "A lot of people are going to be killed for a lie."

"You're right. We're launching a war on a lie. But everybody's going to die some day. And at least we're getting rid of Saddam Hussein. The Iraqis will be grateful."

The good news is that Joe Wilson and his glamorous wife, Valerie Plame, became heroes in a movie.

# Chapter 4. I Go to the President's Press Conference

I was determined to go to the president's press conference after he started the war. I would ask some blunt questions. Presto cautioned me. "Don't get me in trouble. Keep your mouth shut and just listen."

The president said: "We will find the nucular [sic] material. Ya know, it's just a matter of time."

I raised my hand. Another reporter was recognized.

"Where's the proof?"

"The Iraqis tried to buy aluminum tubes in Nigeria [sic] with stuff in them to make nucular [sic] weapons."

I suppressed my need to throw up until I got to the bathroom. In the next stall Joe Wilson was throwing up too.

# Chapter 5. Katrina

Presto and I went to New Orleans for a little R and R. I was accosted by a blond woman in the street. She said, "Come with me."

I was curious, so I went. "I need money," she said.

Fortunately, I had money, so I gave it to her. I always like to help people in need.

Then she took my clothes off. I didn't mind getting comfortable. Then she took her clothes off. I started to feel uncomfortable. She took hold of me, and before I knew what was happening, it was happening. I admit that I felt much better.

Afterwards the wind started to blow. I went out and found Presto at a bar. "It's a hurricane, he said. "We'd better get out of here."

The streets started to fill up with water. I heard somebody shouting something about the levees crumbling.

Most black people couldn't pay the bus fare to get out. We approached a bridge that led to a white city. Blacks were trying to cross. We joined a terrific logjam. Police were firing into the crowd trying to keep us back. I saw two black men shot dead.

We walked into a house along with several other people. When the water flooded the first floor, we went up to the second floor. Then we had to go to the roof.

When the sun came out, we saw that New Orleans was underwater.

We hailed a man with a boat. I took out my money and he let us get on board and ride out of town with him.

Presto said, "They'll be rescued in the next several days."

"I don't see any action."

"New Orleans is too crowded, anyway," said Presto.

"That's a terrible attitude."

"I'm a realist," he replied.

# Chapter 6. Death

I could not bear the indifference to people. I thought that death had won over life. I imagined kindly death coming to heal.

> We walk among the bodies, the stench, you and I walk . . .
> I have come for you. I care.
> You poor, you black. I give you preferred treatment never given in life.
> Black women, I give you preferred treatment.
> Little babies, I give you preferred treatment.
> You poor and sick, I give you preferred treatment.
> I am here to help.
>
> I visit the hospitals. I visit the houses. I visit the doomed city.
> I care about you.
> I take care of the poor, the outcasts.
> The last in line shall be first.
> I cannot bear the heat. I cannot bear the stench. Come with me
> in the cool shade.
> Come with me.
> Come with me.

# Chapter 7. I Meet Kurt Vonnegut

I went into the Gotham Bar and Grill in Manhattan for dinner and saw Kurt Vonnegut sitting alone at a table. As I passed, I said, "Hello, how are you?"

"Terrible," he answered. "I can't smoke in here. I got addicted as a youth."

"I read that."

"You read my stuff?"

"*Slaughterhouse Five, Mother Night* . . ."

"Have a seat. Maybe you can take my mind off smoking for a few minutes."

I did.

"Why are you so down on *Homo sapiens*?"

"Because we are hopeless fools mostly good at mass slaughter. What other animal wrecks the whole joint? Evolution made a mistake. We are fixing that. Soon we will just be a cosmic afterthought. Let the porpoises take over."

"I know some kind people."

"Sure. Babies who are recruited to kill each other by psychopaths at the top. How kind were they when they firebombed Dresden, atomized Hiroshima and Nagasaki, or blew up a whole country like Iraq because a psychopath told them to?"

"Plenty of people protest."

"After the babies are slaughtered. Protests are always

too late. Can you imagine a sign at the Pentagon that says, 'Blessed are the peacemakers?'"

"You think we're hopeless?"

"There's not a chance in hell of Americans becoming humane and reasonable. Leaders are power-drunk chimpanzees. My apologies to the chimpanzees. The earth is a lunatic asylum. We're killing our own life-support system, planet earth."

"The good guys are not all dead yet."

"During the Great Depression and World War II, I dreamed of people becoming humane and reasonable. My dream became a nightmare. People dull the pain with religion. I'm OK with that. What is life all about? I'm damned if I know."

"Surely decent people will eventually get together."

"I'll be dead by then. Send me a telegram."

"I'll send you a telegram. But I think I'll start with a drink right now."

# Chapter 8. I Meet Einstein

I found myself in Princeton and was determined to sit at the feet of Albert Einstein and learn. I walked into a seminar and there he was with chalk in hand standing in front of a blackboard. When he was finished talking, I managed to walk out with him.

I asked, "Leaving equations aside, what is your ultimate goal?"

"I want to know God's thoughts. The rest are details."

"How do you accomplish that?"

"Get beyond the appearance of reality. The appearance of reality is a mere illusion."

"I think we're walking down the street. Isn't that reality?"

"Just a small part of reality. We don't perceive most of reality. People who believe in physics know that the distinction between past, present, and future is only a stubbornly persistent illusion."

"You have confused me."

"Then you should think about practical things like war and peace."

"I'm aware of that."

"Are you aware of the fact that we are a part of the universe that has become aware of itself? We know that's a fact, but we don't know the meaning of that fact. The mystery is what we call God."

"I thought you were an atheist."

"I am struck with awe of the wondrous unknown. That I call God."

"Do you then believe in many universes beyond our ken? What do you think of dark energy and dark matter?"

"What are you talking about?"

"I myself don't know. But if you had a powerful enough telescope, could you see the back of your head from light that had traveled around the entire universe?"

"Why should I bother when it is much simpler to see the back of my head by looking into a mirror and holding another mirror in my hand at an angle behind my head?"

"I'm aware of that."

"If you're aware of that, then the next step is to fall in love. Even chemistry and physics can't explain such an important biological phenomenon as love."

"I'm already in love, and I can explain it."

Then I heard a voice saying, "Wake up, Candide, wake up. You've been babbling in your sleep."

I yawned and rubbed my eyes. Standing at the foot of my bed was Cunegonde!

# Chapter 9. Connie's Misadventures in Afghanistan, Israel, and Palestine

Connie went on a medical mission to Afghanistan. I lost touch with her for several months. Then I heard that she had been taken prisoner by the Taliban. A few days later I received an email saying, "I just arrived in Israel and will be home soon."

At the airport I said, "Connie, the last I heard, you were a prisoner of the Taliban. How did you escape?"

"I escaped with the help of a sympathetic Pashtun woman. Her husband was one of twenty-five men who captured me. The Pashtun woman was twenty. Her husband was sixty. She was forced into marriage. He beat her. She sought revenge by giving me a burka and escorting me out of the camp while the men slept. She begged me to tell the world about the suffering of Afghan women."

After a long embrace, I asked, "How did you get back to the United States?"

"I was conducted through an underground railroad to Kabul where I went to the American embassy. I received a passport and boarded a plane leaving for Israel. In Tel Aviv our embassy put me up with a kind family until arrangements could be made for me to fly home.

"I decided to go to Gaza. Conditions there are terrible. The place is bombed to pieces. Men walk around without jobs. People wear rags. Food and water are short. Hatred of Israelis is universal. They have taken the land of the Palestinians. Every girl and boy wants to grow up to be a martyr."

"How could you stand it there?"

"I couldn't. I left after a day."

"Israel is different?"

"So different. For the affluent, plenty to eat and drink. Beautiful buildings and streets. Educated people. Terrible hatred of Palestinians. Hatred to the death. They have taken the biblical land of the Israelis. So many boys and girls want to grow up to be soldiers."

"No exceptions?"

"Yes. A few exceptions on each side.

"But. But. A quarter of the residents of Israel are poor. More than a third of the children live in poverty. More than half of the poor are Arabs. As I left, 150,000 Israelis were demonstrating to protest the high cost of housing and education, and the low level of salaries. All is not well in the promised land."

"The Israelis sing, 'With eyes turned toward the East, looking toward Zion, then our hope, the two-thousand-year-old hope, will not be lost.'

"The Palestinians sing, 'With the determination of my nature in the land of struggle, Palestine is my home, Palestine is my fire.'"

"Are they not all human beings who can live together?" We looked at each other. We had said these words in unison.

# Chapter 10. I Meet the First Black President

Presto called me on my cell phone and told me that the president was going to Des Moines to have a burger and a Coke at a place named Fast Food. I got on a plane and showed up at Fast Food for lunch. The place was crowded with ordinary people, as the press likes to call them.

The president arrived and ordered a burger and a Coke. He chewed and sipped as the folks asked questions.

A woman eating a burger and drinking a Coke spoke up. "Mr. President, I voted for you. I didn't expect you to give tax cuts to the rich."

"We're in a tough situation. Republicans have taken the middle class hostage. I've got to be realistic. It's tax cuts for everybody or it's nothing."

"But Mr. President," said a man putting down his burger and his Coke. "The rich own almost everything. Now they want more and you're giving it to them. We're paying ransom for the middle class. That ain't fair."

"Look, I'm not giving it to them. They're taking it. Let's get real. I'm for raising taxes on the rich, but I can't do it now. I have to compromise. If I don't, the middle class will get nothing."

I ventured a question. "You saved the bankers. What about saving the unemployed?"

"I'm working on it. I can't change the country overnight."

A waitress ventured a comment. "My husband is in Afghanistan. I don't know why." The bartender said, "Why don't we spend all those billions at home?"

"You know we're pulling out. We're trying to leave a stable government there the way we did in Iraq. You know it all takes time."

I left Fast Food with a better understanding of the president. I didn't feel good about it.

# Chapter 11. I Slip Into and Out of Iran

Presto has an assignment in Iran. He had a way of slipping across the border and getting to Tehran. I could go if I wore a chador and didn't say a word. All right. It's a deal. I wanted to see for myself. As we approached the border, I put on the chador and kept my mouth shut. We were met by several covert CIA operatives and driven to the capital.

It happened that there was a great demonstration against the regime the day we arrived in Tehran. A hundred thousand men and women were walking through the boulevards shouting slogans against tyranny.

The police lobbed tear gas canisters at the marchers. Truncheons were flying. Shots rang out. I was standing five feet from a young woman walking away from the crowd. Suddenly she fell to the ground. Her blood stained her clothes. Her friends cried, "Neda, Neda!" "It burns," she said and died. Hundreds, then thousands of people had the name Neda on their lips. An innocent young woman, not even a demonstrator, was killed.

"Those bastards," I said, violating my oath of silence. "How can I be silent?"

"Let's get out of here," said Presto.

# Chapter 12. I See What's Going On in China

"China's the next part of your curriculum," said Presto. "We'll go along with an American trade delegation."

We arrived in Shanghai in June. Amazing skyscrapers, amazing streets, amazing stores, amazing well-dressed people. We stayed at the amazing Hilton Beijing Hotel. *Ni hao.* Not the China of yesterday.

Presto went to a conference. I went to the university. I wandered into the recreation room. About thirty students were engrossed in their computer screens. Several looked up and welcomed me. "What are we playing?" I asked.

"We're playing hack into the official files of the secret police," one student answered in almost perfect English.

"That sounds like a dangerous game."

"Our job is to expose the rampant corruption in high places."

Just then the police charged into the rec room and arrested everybody, including me, and confiscated the computers, including my BlackBerry.

"I'm an American," I said.

"Tough," said the policeman, who understood the word "tough."

When we got to the interrogation room, I sat across from a man in plain clothes who looked at me without speaking. I took out my bag of renminbi and handed him a fistful of bills.

"You are free to go," he said.

"What about my BlackBerry?" I asked.

He looked at me without speaking.

I looked back at him. Then I handed him another fistful of bills.

"Your BlackBerry also free to go," he said, handing it back to me.

# Chapter 13. I See What's Going On in Russia

"We're off to Moscow on another trade mission," said Presto. "Try to keep out of trouble."

"*Konechno*, of course," I replied, using one of the few words of Russian I knew.

We flew to Sheremetyevo Airport on a sunny day in July. Red Square looked just as I expected, like the pictures I've seen.

Presto went off to a meeting. I hung around Red Square near the Metropole Hotel, where we were staying.

A young man came up to me and asked, "Exchange dollars?"

"*Nyet, spasiba*, no thanks," I answered.

I came upon a small crowd listening to a speaker. I learned that it was a political rally of an opposition party.

Soon I heard the ululations of police vans approaching.

They stopped and the whole crowd was pushed into the vans, including me. I heard somebody say, "Illegal meeting." Every unofficial meeting is illegal.

After two days in a cell, I was led to a small room to appear before a magistrate. I protested that I was just listening, that I didn't understand Russian, and furthermore, I'm an American.

"It's illegal to listen," the magistrate said. "Very serious."

"What will it take to clear up this mess?" I asked.

The magistrate shrugged his shoulders.

I took out my bag of money and pulled out a handful of rubles, which I put on the table.

"Case dismissed," said the magistrate.

The next day I heard that all the fingers of the speaker at the rally had somehow gotten broken.

I went back to Moscow several years later. This time the demonstrators filled Red Square. Interesting. I saw the man with the broken fingers in the crowd.

# Chapter 14. I Get a Job in Finance

Presto said, "I think you should get a job. See what it's like to have responsibility, make money."

"I'm ready," I replied.

"My brother-in-law Agresso is CEO of a hedge fund, Intensive Care Investments. I'll give him a call and see if he has an opening for you."

"Agreed."

Presto made the arrangements. I arrived at a plush Wall Street office Monday morning and was ushered in to talk with Agresso.

"I'm going to teach you the business, Candide," he said. "Start by going to each department to watch. Ask questions."

After three months I had made the rounds. Investing seemed pretty easy to me.

Then Agresso sent me to the stock exchange floor to observe. Another two months. Then I became a trader for six months, placing my own bets with other people's money.

After another nine months placing bets with larger amounts of money, Agresso put his arm around my shoulder and said in an intimate tone, "Look here, Candide, the housing market is way overleveraged. It's about to crash. Mortgage-backed securities will become worthless. I'm selling them to our customers and using the money to buy commodities like gold. When the housing market collapses, we pay our customers a few cents on the dollar and we're left with the difference."

Well, Agresso was right. The mortgage market collapsed and I had made a fabulous amount of money by making a few phone calls to wealthy investors.

"Do you think it was right to tell your customers that the market was going up, up, up? Buy, buy, buy? Basically we fleeced them."

"Don't be too hard on yourself, Candide. They expected the market to go up, we expected the market to go down."

"But you encouraged them to believe that the market was going up when you knew that it was about to go down."

"These investors are autonomous individuals who can think for themselves. It's their responsibility to think for themselves."

"But we misled them. Don't you think we have a responsibility too?"

"Listen, Candide. You and I didn't make the world the way it is. The prudent man accepts reality. I am unashamed."

I was troubled by all this. At the same time I was a lot richer.

## Chapter 15. I Visit Walter Reed Memorial Hospital

I took it upon myself to visit Walter Reed Memorial Hospital using my press credentials to get in. I saw misery and courage. All the patients were gamely trying to get rehabilitated and become civilians again. Except patients whose minds were so shattered that they can never be rehabilitated. They will be tormented for the rest of their lives for what they saw, what they did, and what was done to them.

I talked with an army sergeant. I'll call him Sergeant Jones. His arms were blown off up to the elbows and his legs were blown off up to his knees by a roadside bomb in Iraq. He was practicing using prosthetic arms and legs. I had trouble controlling my emotions when we talked.

"I can see it's hard."

"Yeah, it's hard. But I am what I am. I have no choice."

"You were Medevaced out?"

"Yeah, I lost consciousness. There was a lot of blood. I could have died. But here I am, not as good as new. But alive instead of dead."

"How long will it take you to learn how to use these devices?"

"It varies from one person to another. You can't get discouraged. But we all do. Then we get over it. Some, anyway."

"Will you eventually get a job?"

"Yeah. I can work a computer. I can answer a phone. I'll be able to walk around. Not run, I suppose."

"Are you married? Have you children?"

"No and no. Some woman will have to see that there's a man behind these devices. I have thoughts and feelings. I can love and be loved. Some woman out there will realize that. I hope."

"Are you bitter?"

"No. Yes. I fought in a great cause. But shit, this is a high price to pay. I don't diss the army. I volunteered for a great cause. That validates me. But shit, this is a high price to pay."

"And look at my medals," he added, sticking his chest out a bit.

And then he cried.

# Chapter 16. Genocide in the Congo

Presto had gotten an assignment from the CIA to go to the Congo, make an on-site inspection, and report back. I had read on the Internet that six nations were involved in the war and that several hundred thousand Hutus and Tutsis had been killed by troops and ragtag militias. Several hundred thousand more had died from dehydration, starvation, and disease. I decided to go and see for myself. Connie and Martin, her favorite teacher at medical school, and Maria, her friend and classmate, went with me.

Our plane landed in the capital, Kinshasa. We drove a jeep into the countryside to a refugee camp. At several sites along the way we saw piles of dead bodies.

At the camp, we saw another pile of dead bodies. A woman who spoke a little English came up to us. She was about 30.

"I Tutsi," she said. "Hutu and Tutsi kill other. All. Men, women, children." She paused to weep.

"Hutu men — clubs, guns, machetes — come our camp at night. I hold hands my little boy and girl. They pulled from hands and slashed with machetes. I run. Cry. Fall face down. Pretend dead. Screaming women raped. Then killed. Hundreds fall. Die. Dead on top me. Screaming men, women, children clubbed, shot, hacked. Dead. I lie in pool blood. Men go away. I get up. Need water. Please. Please."

We gave her a liter bottle of water. Tears streamed down her face. "What I do? Where I go?"

We saw hundreds of other figures moving aimlessly, dazed.

Tears streamed down our faces too. Even Presto's. We could save only one woman. We drove her back to Kinshasa and left her at a guarded refugee camp.

I said, "'Never again.' Remember that? After the Holocaust, then came Rwanda, Darfur, Kosovo, Bosnia, Cambodia, Sudan. What have I forgotten?"

"Why didn't we do something?" asked Connie.

"We certainly knew what was coming," said Martin.

"Are we not complicit?" asked Maria.

Presto explained. We have complicated alliances with different countries. When we get involved, we alienate allies. Could make the situation worse.

How can a situation be worse than the murder and starvation of a million people? It cannot be worse. A warning, a blockage of funds, a show of force could prevent this madness before it starts. Those are my thoughts.

"It's very remote from the concerns of the public," said Presto.

"But our leaders know about these impending slaughters before they start. Why don't they alert the public?"

"Who, this party or that party?" asked Presto. "One side will blame the other if we spend money trying to keep people from tearing each other apart."

"Oh, sure," said Martin. "Unless it's Afghanistan or Iraq, where we do the killing."

"You sound cynical," answered Presto.

"I am cynical. Why profess to be pious and say 'Never again'? I am cynical about cynicism."

# Chapter 17. The Miner Rescue in Chile

"I have an assignment in Chile," said Presto. "We're leaving tomorrow morning." Connie, Martin, and Maria decided to come along.

The day we arrived in Santiago, thirty-three miners were trapped in a cave-in at the San José copper and gold mine in the Atacama Desert, near Copiapó. We flew down to get a firsthand look.

A big team of rescuers assembled around the mine entrance. They worked furiously to drill boreholes down 2,300 feet to reach the miners.

The miners struggled against heat and humidity. They rationed food and water. They organized themselves under the leadership of Luis Urzua, the shift leader. He assigned areas for sleeping, washing, and working. He assigned specialized tasks to each miner, with the consent of all. Discipline kept up hope against all odds.

The rescue site on the ground became known as Camp Hope—Campamento Esperanza. Family members and specialists established their own division of labor. As physicians, Connie, Martin, and Maria pitched in.

On the seventeenth day a borehole reached the cave. Then a second and a third. They were divided to send down oxygen, food, water, and video cameras. I joined in and helped the families prepare food.

Then we hoped that a rescue capsule would reach the miners without mishap. The capsule, named Fénix—Phoenix—was built with the help of NASA. It had enough room for one man. At last it was winched down and the first miner was brought up. The capsule contained sunglasses, oxygen masks, a heart monitor, and video cameras. One by one, after sixty-nine days, all thirty-three miners were rescued. Some were sick. Most were amazingly well. The president of Chile announced Misión Cumplida Chile, Mission Accomplished Chile.

For sixty-nine days, the whole world watched, then breathed a sigh of relief.

"Why such attention, why such euphoria?" I asked Presto.

"First, the miners were not enemies," said Presto. "They could not be vilified.

"Second, the predicament of the miners was easy to imagine, so it was easy to sympathize with them.

"Third," he said, "the media kept our attention fixed on the day-to-day events. We were present in mind and spirit."

"Well," I said, "thousands of American troops have been killed in Iraq and Afghanistan. They cannot be vilified."

"They are not," he answered.

"The death of each soldier is easy to imagine," I said.

"Yes," said Presto. "But not the death of thousands. They become anonymous deaths.

"I'm sure you will ask about the media. They only rarely

fix our attention on individual deaths in war. After a while, thousands of deaths become background noise. Our generals want thousands of deaths to become background noise. Then the public is less moved to interfere with their military plans."

"This is monstrous," I interjected.

"That's the way the world works," replied Presto.

Still, Connie, Martin, Maria, and I rejoiced over this small victory. Well, not so small.

# Chapter 18. Langley Air Force Base

We went to the Langley Air Force Base in Virginia to see how the drone operation was proceeding. A drone, I learned, is a pilotless airplane flown by electronic instructions. The technology is so marvelous that the operator at Langley can instruct the plane to bomb our enemies in Afghanistan and Pakistan from the distance of 10,000 miles.

Presto mentioned information overload. "What is that?" I asked.

"The personnel at Langley are getting so much information that they can't sort it all out. A lot of information comes in but isn't studied in time."

"In time for what?"

"In time to decide where to drop bombs."

"So?"

"So we sometimes drop bombs on innocent civilians before we have time to determine that they are innocent. They are mistaken for the enemy."

"That's criminal," I said.

"We are fighting in a good cause against Al Qaeda and the Taliban. The innocent men, women, and children who have been killed as a result of information overload at Langley Air Force Base have given their lives for a good cause."

"They have not given their lives. Their lives have been taken."

"All the same."

"Why don't we at least assign more people to look at the information before we act on it?"

"We are stretched very thin. If we assigned more people at Langley, we would still be short of people on the ground. From a drone, sometimes a wedding party looks like a Taliban meeting. We don't have enough people on the ground to check it out."

"So we kill the members of the wedding party?"

"At least they all die happy."

"Not amusing, Presto. Won't the taking of innocent lives turn the world against us? If so, we will lose the battle for freedom. We will accomplish the opposite of what we intended."

"Of course not," said Presto. "Everybody knows that we are the greatest force for good in the world."

"That may be true. But people might lose sight of that fact and become distracted by the bloodshed caused by our battle for good."

# Chapter 19. Murder in Tucson

Presto mentioned to me that he had some business in Tucson, Arizona, so I packed my bag and we flew out of New York.

As we drove past a shopping mall, we heard some shots ring out and saw people falling to the ground.

By the time we drove into the parking lot, six people had been killed, including a nine-year-old girl, and thirteen more had been wounded. We learned that Congresswoman Gabrielle Giffords had been holding a "Congress on Your Corner" meeting outside a Safeway food market and a crazy man with a Glock pistol with a thirty-three-round magazine had fired on the meeting. Representative Giffords was lying on the ground with a bullet through her head.

We ran toward the crowd. By the time we got there several people had pinned down the crazy man on the ground and a bystander had grabbed a second magazine of thirty-three rounds. Others were trying to stanch blood running from the wounded. Everybody acted spontaneously to help.

I was so stunned I could hardly speak.

"How could this man buy a gun and magazines that hold thirty-three bullets?" I yelled.

Even Presto was shaken. "When politicians incite people to carry guns and treat their political opponents as enemies, some people are going to take them literally and start shooting."

"Most people hate this inflammatory rhetoric and look what it has led to."

"Most people aren't organized. They can't do anything about it," said Presto. "They are stirred up for a few weeks, shocked, angry, then forget. Too busy with the mundane. Until the next time."

"On the contrary. We are pierced with grief as one large family. It will never heal."

I couldn't get the image of the dead girl out of my mind and didn't want to. Some words lamenting the death of children ran through my mind.

I often think: they have just gone out,
and now will be coming back home.
The day is fine, don't be dismayed.
They have just gone for a long walk.

Ah, *Totenkinderlieder*. So you say, Gustav Mahler. But our hearts are broken beyond repair as was yours.

# Chapter 20. The Disaster in Japan

Connie, Martin, and Maria were in Japan with a medical delegation when the earthquake and tsunami struck along the northeast coast. They were attending a conference in the earthquake zone and I couldn't get a response to my email. I was terrified. Even more when I learned that three nuclear power plants were threatened.

After four days of anxiety, Connie responded.

"We are grieving for the lives we lost. We were in the midst of helping patients at the Takata hospital when we felt severe shaking. Fifteen minutes later a wall of water as high as the four-story building smashed into us. The doctors and nurses brought patients to the roof, hoping that the hospital would not collapse. We left many old and sick behind. No time! No time! My head is full of screams. Those on the roof survived. I am wrenching with grief because I let others die, and I did not die.

"Cars, boats, buildings are strewn like broken toys. Bodies lie everywhere as if sudden sleep overcame them. The living move aimlessly here and there. I am a drop in a sea of grief.

"All of Takata and many towns around were destroyed. Now we fear radiation dispersed from the ruined nuclear power plants.

"I remember a doctor on the first floor of the hospital, just before he was engulfed by the rush of water, who threw his satellite phone to another doctor near the stairs so that we could call for help. Peace to him."

# Chapter 21. Blacks Out of Work

I went for an interview with a black correspondent. I am not authorized to use his name. We went to see a black family in Philadelphia.

Several people were sitting around a kitchen table. A woman in her sixties was having treatment for breast cancer. She lost her job at a bank when she got sick. Her husband lost his job as a long-distance truck driver after working for the same company for thirty-five years. He had been looking for another job as a truck driver for two years but couldn't find one. Twenty people showed up for every job opening. So he got part-time work as a dishwasher at Red Lobster. He and his wife didn't have enough to pay their mortgage so they lost their home.

Another woman at the table was working on and off as a nursing assistant. She had to sleep in her car.

Another woman said, "This is how it is in this neighborhood. We're struggling every day. And it's getting harder."

My friend the correspondent said, "I go all around the country. It's this way everywhere."

I thought, I'm doing so well, and so many people are struggling as if we're living in a third-world country.

Strange. A majority *are* living in a third-world country while a small minority are living in a first-world country. We're moving backwards.

# Chapter 22. Migrant Farm Workers

I had heard that the leader of the migrant farm workers' union had responded to hostility by inviting non-migrant farm workers to go out in the fields and find out what it is like to pick lettuce, berries, and grapes under the blazing sun. Illegal immigrants are taking your jobs? Come out to the farms and, welcome, take your jobs back.

I decided to investigate. I flew out to Salinas Valley, California. At dawn I hopped on a truck of migrants and drove out to a farm. There I joined a group of about fifty workers picking lettuce. Men, women, and children were working when I arrived. A few other non-farm workers had joined in. Everybody was very friendly.

After about an hour of bending over to pick the lettuce, the pain in my back started getting to me. I was also drenched in sweat from the hundred-degree heat. Into the second hour, I became dizzy and had to sit down and drink and drink and drink. I already had a much better understanding of migratory farm workers. Long hours, hard work, hot sun, low pay. Forget about it. The question was, how to get back to town.

I was working next to a man named José. His wife and three children were working alongside him. I was surprised when José offered to drive me some fifty miles round trip.

"You'll lose more than an hour's work," I said. "That's too big a sacrifice to make."

"Don't worry. You need help. I'll help you."

So we drove back to my hotel. With his little English and my little Spanish, I learned that he and his family were "illegal," a fact that seemed irrelevant at the moment. I offered him fifty dollars for his time, gas, and just because he was such a good guy.

"No," he said. "This is from my heart to someone who wanted to learn about the life of migratory farm workers. It's not a matter of money."

We hugged goodbye and I managed to slip a fifty-dollar bill in his pocket without his noticing it.

When I checked out the next morning, the clerk handed me an envelope. Inside was my fifty-dollar bill with a note that said, "When I need help, you help me. When you need help, I help you. José."

# Chapter 23. A Narrow Escape in Libya

Presto informed me that we were going to Libya on a secret Special Ops mission. Boots on the ground, so to speak. I was to take no notes. We weren't supposed to be there.

We landed in Benghazi and drove overland to Tripoli. Gaddafi loyalists still controlled the city center and the Gaddafi compound. We arrived just in time to hear a rant from the dictator himself. I had no idea what he was saying, but the crowd roared in approval.

It happened that I carried a handgun in a holster secured to my belt. Not even Presto knew it, because the whole contraption was covered by my jacket.

The thought entered my head: I'm standing within a hundred feet of the monster Gaddafi. What if I put a bullet through his heart? That would be the end of a madman. But then I would be lynched.

As I was thinking these thoughts, I put my hand on my pistol, undecided what to do.

Instantly two burly men grabbed my arms, grabbed the gun, and knocked me to the ground. They dragged me off, threw me in a car, and drove to an abandoned warehouse on the outskirts of the city.

They pulled me out of the car, marched me to a side door of the warehouse, and pushed me inside.

I could hardly see anything. After my eyes adjusted to the

semi-darkness, I saw about a hundred men sitting around on the concrete floor talking in Arabic. The stench was terrible. Someone who spoke a little English came up to me and said, "No water. No food. Sit. We die."

I was too agitated to sit, so I walked around, stepping in excrement and urine, getting madly thirsty and hungry as the hours went by.

I looked around for a way to escape. All the other men in this hellhole had already looked. I thought, this is it.

After two days, the side door was suddenly thrown open. Someone on the outside yelled something. Everyone moved toward the door and ran outside. So did I. The two men who had forced me into this tomb grabbed me in great agitation. One yelled, "Gaddafi gone. We free. You free. Praise Allah. Thank you, thank you, American."

I was pretty disoriented for a moment. I felt as if I was in a theater where the actors suddenly threw off their sinister masks and put on happy ones.

I was driven to the American embassy. Presto was waiting for me. He gave me a little lecture about being a premature revolutionary.

# Chapter 24. The Hundred-Year-Old Man

I got on the train from New York to Washington and sat down next to a gray-bearded old man who looked very sad. I happened to be reading *Night* by Elie Wiesel. "I can tell you all about that. My name is Isaac. I am Jewish. I only live at night. During the day I am dead.

"I was born in Odessa. My father was killed at the front in the Great War. I was eight years old. My mother scrambled to support my two younger sisters and me by opening a small shop that sold dry goods.

"We lived through twenty-one years of deprivation accompanied by heroic communist slogans. My sisters and I married and we each had three children. Then war resumed and I was drafted, only to retreat to the steppes. My mother, my wife, my three children, my two sisters, and their six children were rounded up by the Nazis, sent to concentration camps, and pushed into the gas chambers. I, the soldier, am the only survivor.

"From those days to this I have been dead. But by night all my family is alive and I am alive. I converse with my mother, my wife, my children, my sisters, all of them. We have parties, we go on outings into the countryside, we look at the blue sky and the white clouds and the green earth and we are happy. I ask, can this be true? I touch my wife's hand, I embrace my daughters. It is true. They are alive, thank God.

"Then I wake up, dead. I wait for the next night and the next and the next. When I wake up in the morning, I wish for real death, the death of nothingness, death without torment. Why have I been cursed with the life and death of one hundred years? Can you tell me? Why have I been so cursed? Can you tell me?"

# Chapter 25. Candide Is Sentenced to Death

"My beloved Connie," he cried as he heard the guilty verdict.

"Candide is innocent!" Connie shouted in the courtroom.

"Enough," said the judge, "or you will be escorted out."

The judge concluded a long statement. "You have been charged with first degree murder for taking the lives of two innocent people. Your fingerprints were found on the detonator that set off the bomb. The evidence is conclusive. I sentence you to death."

Uproar. Then his lawyer rose.

"Your honor," his lawyer said, "my client would like to make a statement."

"Proceed," said the judge.

Candide calmly stood before the court. "If this is to be my fate, so be it. Here is what I believe."

Not in death raining from the skies.
Not in death from the point of a gun.
Not in death from hatred.
Not in death from vengeance.
Not in death from want.

Let us cultivate our garden.
Our garden, the entire earth.
The earth that belongs to us all.

The earth that keeps us all.
The earth that sustains us all.

Let us learn.
It is not too late.
I believe you who live
will see our garden blossom.

Just then, a breathless man entered the court. "Your honor, your honor," he shouted. "I must speak."

"Remove that man from the court," ordered the judge.

"This man is innocent."

"Come forward, then."

The man approached the bench. He took a cell phone out of his pocket. He showed the judge a video that he had taken from a distance. It showed a man about to detonate a bomb. Another man ran up and struggled with him. But too late. The other man was Candide. In grabbing the detonator, his fingerprints left their mark.

The judge explained what he saw. The courtroom was in an uproar. The judge gaveled for quiet. "This man is not a murderer. He is a hero. He is innocent. The verdict is void. I declare a mistrial." He repeated, "The verdict is void."

Connie and Candide fell into each other's arms and rejoiced. They went to a justice of the peace and got married.

Presto declared that Candide's apprenticeship was over.

Candide's mother and father threw a celebratory party

at their fifteen-thousand-square-foot mansion on their twenty-acre park in Greenwich and invited 250 people, none of whom Candide or Connie knew.

| 2011 |

*Prose*

# God Is Guilty

I recently had a conversation with a friend of mine who is a member of the clergy. I cannot mention his name because he is not authorized to speak to anyone about the subject in question. No, that is not exactly true. He is afraid of being disgraced and losing his job if his name is associated with the conversation that he had with me.

First, I can tell you he was a pious young man who wanted to express his piety by leading a congregation. As he matured, he started to ask questions about the biblical God. Why all the mercilessness? Throwing Adam and Eve out of the Garden of Eden because they wanted knowledge? Allowing Cain to kill Abel because God accepted Abel's burnt offerings but not Cain's, causing an insane rage in Cain? Forcing Abraham to kill his son Isaac but staying his hand at the last second? Killing innocent firstborn Egyptians because of Pharaoh's stubbornness? Inciting Moses to kill thousands of his followers in the desert and inflicting communicable diseases on thousands of others? Allowing Joshua to slaughter all the innocent inhabitants of Jericho except for the family of a harlot who hid Joshua's spy? Turning Lot's wife into a pillar of salt because she wanted to take a last look at her hometown, Sodom? Tormenting Job and killing his innocent sons and daughters? Killing everybody on Earth, even the babies — again the babies — except Noah and his family? Allowing Jesus Christ, his son, not just any-body, to be crucified? And throughout post-biblical histo-ry, countenancing hundreds of millions of deaths through wars, genocides, starvation, dehydration, and disease? If this were the work of the devil, my friend could understand it. But the work of God, who is said to operate in mysteri-ous ways beyond the understanding of man? These are not mysteries. They are crimes.

My friend, whose name I cannot mention — I would never betray him — began to have horrible hallucinations when he slept, torn apart by his desire to believe in God while agoniz-ing over God's perpetration or countenancing of such hor-rible deeds.

One night he went to bed, and before he fell asleep, God entered his bedroom.

"I know what you're thinking," said God.

"No doubt you do. I have lost faith. You created humans and you have visited catastrophes on them. You are no better than the devil."

"Well, Jim . . . " (I'm using the name Jim, but that's not his real name), "Well, Jim, there is no such thing as the devil. The devil is a figment of human imagination."

Jim put aside his doubts on that subject and then went through the whole list of biblical atrocities listed above, and recited a great deal of mankind's bloody history and asked, "How can I forgive you?"

"You must understand," answered God, "that I don't

control human actions. I am not responsible for anything that happens on Earth."

"But you made humans in your image. I used to think that your image glowed with goodness. Forgive me for saying so, but it does not. It glows with evil."

"You must understand," answered God, "that I created the universe 13.75 billion years ago. I should say universes. But let's talk about the one you know. Your universe evolved from the Big Bang—of course you don't know what happened before that—your universe evolved and eventually produced self-replicating creatures that in turn evolved into humans. My aim 13.75 billion years ago was to create decent human beings, but you must admit that it is hard to plan ahead 13.75 billion years and I made some slight miscalculations and you have humans as they are and you can't blame me."

"But if you can create entire universes, why couldn't you get at least one universe right?"

"You don't know what's right and wrong with the other universes. You are just coming to understand that other universes exist because they cause the accelerating expansion of your universe and you call those forces dark energy and dark matter, which doesn't explain much.

"Let me tell you, I am only the servant of a greater force that is as mysterious to me as I am to you. I don't understand anything beyond the universes, but there is much more beyond those universes and I have no idea what it is."

"My God! You are almost as helpless as human beings," exclaimed Jim.

"Not quite," answered God.

"Let me try to think this through. You made a slight miscalculation 13.75 billion years ago. The deed is done. Humans are what they are, or rather what we are."

"That's right."

"So we humans have to work things out for ourselves."

"That's right."

"So if we are to be just, fair, and merciful, it's up to us humans to work it out ourselves."

"That's right."

"Nothing can mitigate the fact that you screwed up."

"That's right."

"Except us."

"That's right."

"You have certainly put a big burden on us."

"Yes, I have. Unwittingly."

"God knows if we can handle it."

"No he doesn't."

"All we can do is try."

"I'd feel much better if you did. You can help me get off the hook."

"How much time do we have?"

"I don't know. Remember, I'm subordinate to a force greater than myself."

"Then I commit myself to doing the best I can to get us

off the hook. And to get you off the hook. God knows if I can succeed."

"No he doesn't."

That's about where the conversation between Jim — a pseudonym — and God ended. Jim is organizing something. God knows what.

| 2011 |

# Ruthless

Ruth came into a small fortune when she was about thirty due to the generosity of an uncle who remembered her in his will, which was duly probated after he passed away. Ruth is 5'7" tall, blond, pretty, a graduate of Bennington College, lives in New York, and is particularly known for her generosity.

Her parents and younger brother live in Geneva, where her father works for UBS in the derivatives department. So Ruth flew over to discuss what she should do with the money. They jointly decided that Ruth should open an upscale women's clothing store on the fashionable stretch of Fifth Avenue, which would attract wealthy women who were ready and able to spend considerable sums of money for dresses, blouses, skirts, shoes, jewelry, and other accoutrements. Given that Ruth had majored in nineteenth-century English literature, she was hardly qualified to do anything else but run an upscale expensive women's dress shop, except teach or write, neither of which she had any interest in.

She signed a lease for a space at street level in an excellent location, hired a buyer, and with some puffs in the press by fellow English majors at Bennington College, who had gotten into the business of writing for the fashion pages of several metropolitan newspapers due to their mastery of the English language, she opened her shop.

Word soon got around several circles of upper-class women, who were not particularly looking for discounts, that very desirable clothing was available at Ruth's shop. They came and were not disappointed. The news of her excellent taste, or at least that of her buyer, spread around additional circles of upper-class women and soon Ruth had a more than thriving business. She was making a substantial amount of money on the generous markups that are common at this level of merchandise.

By then the word had gotten around among aunts, uncles, cousins, Bennington alumni, acquaintances, and acquaintances of acquaintances that Ruth was, shall we say, rich.

An uncle who had lost his job at a big-box bookstore that had closed came around for money to pay his mortgage. Ruth gladly agreed to help. A cousin who had a new idea for an advanced smartphone needed money for a startup business. Ruth invested. Then friends came with various money problems and Ruth helped them. Soon, complete strangers heard of Ruth's generosity and they came by for help, which Ruth gave them.

Meanwhile, Ruth was receiving mail solicitations from UNICEF, Doctors Without Borders, Human Rights Watch, Mothers Against Drunk Driving, and twenty other worthy causes, all offering return address labels as a gesture of good will for her contributions. Ruth gave with such generosity that she came to the attention of the three judges of the Generosity Award, who traveled to her shop, and with much fanfare, presented her with the award. Following the award, all kinds of down-and-out people started to hang out in Ruth's shop, hoping to catch her eye and come away with some money.

Word started to get around the circles of well-to-do women who shopped at Ruth's clothing salon that a lower class of people was milling around Ruth's shop and the shop was getting dirty and smelly. The fashionable women took their patronage elsewhere and the day came when Ruth couldn't pay the rent. The landlord gave notice to vacate.

The next day, a cousin of Ruth's named Roth—a coincidence in names—came to manage the shop while Ruth took a leave of absence. He was 5'7", had a dark moustache and close-cut beard, wore dark glasses, wore a black fedora pulled down over his forehead, wore a long, loose-fitting black outershirt, and spoke in a deep voice. The first thing he did was to hire a doorman who was instructed to keep the riffraff out. The next thing he did was to hire a cleaning service to get rid of all the debris that lay in the isles as well as the bottles and cups that had accumulated in the fitting rooms. Roth negotiated with the landlord for a postponement of rent payments for two months with a promise to pay in full.

Soon, word got out among fashionable women's circles that Ruth's shop was sparkling clean again.

"Have you heard," Patricia said to Priscilla, "a man named Roth is managing Ruth's shop while she is away and he has made everything sparkling clean again."

"Yes, I have heard," said Priscilla, "and I have told Marlene and Mary Ellen." They in turn told Henrietta and Harriet, who told Beatrice and Buzzy. Soon the shop was buzzing again. The rent was duly paid.

Meanwhile, the aunts, uncles, cousins, Bennington classmates, miscellaneous friends, and hangers-on down to the homeless, who had come off the street to use the facilities and get a handout, grew restive.

"We need Ruth. Where has she gone? Don't you think it's suspicious that she disappeared as soon as Roth showed up? Something fishy is going on here. Roth is ruthless, not at all like Ruth. He seems capable of anything. What do you think he has done with Ruth?"

Several of the aunts, uncles, cousins, hangers-on, as well as the three judges of the Generosity Award, went to the police, who dispatched a detective to look for Ruth. One day he heard a woman's voice coming from a back room of the shop. She was talking on the phone. The detective knocked on the door. He turned the handle and found that the door was locked. "Police. Let me in."

Roth opened the door. "I heard a woman's voice," said the detective. "Where is she?"

"You must be imagining it," replied Roth. "No woman is here."

"I distinctly heard a woman's voice." He looked around and saw no woman. "I don't get it. I think you kidnapped and hid a woman. You'll have to accompany me to the station."

"Very well," said Roth. "If you insist, I will go with you."

The police station was filled with interested parties. The lead interrogator said, "We think there is probable cause to book you for kidnapping."

"No," said Roth. "You are wrong. There is no kidnapping."

"We'd like to know where the shop owner is."

At this point, Roth took off his black fedora, and blond hair came tumbling out. He took off his dark glasses, pulled off his moustache and close-cut beard, took off his long, loose-fitting black outershirt, and the form of a woman appeared. Roth spoke in the voice of a female. "I am Ruth."

The police and the interested parties were astonished at the transformation. "Why? Why?"

"Ruth was too good a woman. She destroyed herself with her generosity. The world does not countenance generosity. Ruth had to become somebody else, somebody hard. You must be hard in order to survive. So Ruth had to become Roth."

She asked:

When will the day come when a woman can be generous?

When will the day come when a man can be good?

When will the day come when selfishness is banished?

When will the day come when ruth prevails?

| 2011 |

# An End to Fighting

My platoon is cramped together on a mountainside over-looking Korengal Valley. Never heard of it before. Godfor-saken place. Northeastern Afghanistan. Cramped together with fleas, flies, and tarantulas too. Supposed to get rid of the Taliban. We aren't.

We see several small villages and scattered clumps of houses.

The Taliban play hide-and-seek. They hide, then run out and shoot at us then hide again.

Some of our guys are wounded. Some are killed. Sorry to say. Between firefights our captain negotiates with the vil-lage elders. Give us information, we give you food, clothes, build a school, a road, whatever you need. They say, you kill us, then you give us candy.

Today fire is coming from a house down in the valley. We see a woman and child in the house. The captain directs fire on different sides hoping the woman and child will run out the other side. They don't.

Well, goddamn it, the Taliban in the house are trying to kill us. The captain calls in an Apache copter. Take out the house. Done. Then to us: Shoot anybody who comes out. No-body. The village elders ask permission to collect the dead. Including the woman and child.

I'm on a path and come eye to eye with, who? I shoot him.

I shoot everything that moves. Except us. Except when we're negotiating.

Today, by which I mean the next day, a detachment from our platoon is sent out on a mission to engage Taliban spotted on the mountainside. Around a bend the platoon is ambushed. The captain sends a rescue team with medics. And me. All our guys are dead except one. One minute he's alive. The next minute he's dead.

Hey, Bill! For Christ's sake!

I'm on Prozac. A guy next to me is having a conversation with himself. Another guy is walking in tight circles.

A senior officer comes to visit and asks, why are we here?

Today my tour ends. Back in the states I remember all this shit. Not remember. Am terrified by. An army shrink says it will take time to get over it.

I stay with my parents in Philadelphia for a while. They want to talk. I can't talk. I'm thinking, how could I have done that?

I visit a high school friend in Newark for a few days. He wants to talk. Can't talk. I'm thinking, how could I have done that?

I'm in New York with a girl, young woman I mean. We do it. It's good. I'm over there again in nightmares. Daymares too. Any such thing? I'm thinking, how could I have done that?

A car horn blasts next to me. I'm terrified. I'm jumping out of my skin. I'm thinking, how could I have done that?

I take more Prozac. It doesn't obliterate the past. I need something to obliterate the past. I'm driven to obliterate the past. How could I have done that? Release me. I'm thinking it. I think I'm yelling it.

Hey, Bill! For Christ's sake!

I go up to the roof of a building on 53rd Street. I look at the pedestrians below. Release me. Release me. I think I'm yelling it. I'm falling into the void.

| 2011 |

# The Voyage of the Titanic

In third class, sometimes known as steerage, a conversation takes place among three women in their twenties.

"Don't you think it merry that three of us are named Kate and we have found each other?"

Second Kate: "It's luck. The luck of the Irish."

Third Kate: "The luck of the Irish Catholic."

First Kate: "Where might you girls be going and why?"

Second Kate: "New York. I'm joining Shannon, my sister. She's got a flat and a nice job. Waitressing."

Third Kate: "Chicago. Saw a help-wanted handbill. Department store, you know. Ladies' work. What about you, Kate?"

First Kate: "Joining my Kevin. Milwaukee. Getting married. Lots of kids I'm hoping. A better life."

Second Kate: "A better life."

Third Kate: "A better life."

First Kate: "Irish Catholics ain't exactly welcome in America, are they? Step warily."

Second Kate: "Ain't welcome. Like Ireland."

Third Kate: "Ha!"

First Kate: "Ha!"

In second class, a party has formed at a dining table.

"I must say, the food is first class even though we're in second class," exclaimed Mrs. Benson.

"Indeed," responded Mr. Bingley. "They have spared nothing on this ship."

"Have you sneaked into first class?" asked Mrs. Lovely.

"Mrs. Lovely and I boldly walked in," declared Mr. Lovely. "We exchanged a greeting with Mr. Benjamin Guggenheim. Cheeky of us, what?"

"Cheeky, indeed," replied Mr. Benson. "Are you going to keep up the acquaintance after we dock in New York?"

"We shall see, Mr. Benson. We shall see."

"J.P. Morgan was expected on board. Had to cancel at the last minute. Illness, I believe," observed Mr. Jones.

"A pity," added Mrs. Jones. "He financed the whole venture, I'm told."

In first class, a group of notables converses by the pool.

Benjamin Guggenheim: "Three days out and Captain Smith is pushing it to get to New York in six days."

John Jacob Astor: "We shall. We shall. The sky is clear. The sea is calm."

Isador Straus: "And Mr. Ismay and Mr. Andrews are pushing the captain. They must set a record, being the owner and designer, you know."

Lady Duff Gordon: "And rightly so. In 1912 we must surpass everything that has gone before. Look what they have put into this ship. A squash court, a Turkish bath, libraries, barber shops. It's a whole world."

Ida Straus: "Isador and I so much enjoy the dining. Champaign, caviar, chateaubriand, peach Melba — the chef has done wonders, wonders!"

Sir Cosmo Duff Gordon: "A whole world, as you say, Lady Gordon. I venture to suppose that third class is the wretched of the earth. Turkish, Italian, Scandinavian, God knows who or what."

Lady Duff Gordon: "And in second class, the second class. In first class, the first class."

Sir Duff Gordon: "Yes. The poor of the earth in steerage. The pushers in second class . . ."

Lady Duff Gordon: "We all get along if they stay where they are."

Mrs. Charlotte Cardoza: "I daresay we have on this ship the highest percentage of millionaires of anyplace."

Molly Brown, wife of the Colorado silver mine king: "I'd say the ship has more millionaires per square foot than Wall Street."

Lady Duff Gordon: "Mrs. Brown, I hope you don't think me rude, but I hear that you entered the gentlemen's smoking lounge yesterday evening and smoked a cigar."

Molly Brown: "I did, indeed. I've had enough of exclusion. Where am I to go to smoke a cigar if not the smoking lounge?"

Lady Duff Gordon: "You will certainly go far, I should think."

Molly Brown: "I have gone far. And I shall go farther."

John Jacob Astor: "We may be getting into some trouble before you go farther."

Molly Brown: "What do you mean?"

John Jacob Astor: "The British, the Germans, and the Russians are arming themselves to the teeth. Recruiting. Building navies. No good can come of it. We're heading for a smashup."

Madeleine Astor: "I hear the band playing. How delightful. Let us go and listen."

In the engine room, two men furiously shovel coal.

"I've worked in the mines. But I've never worked as hard as this."

"Aye, mate. The captain's pushing it as hard as he can."

In the wireless room, an operator talks to a boy.

Operator: "A report of icebergs to the north. Take this message to the captain."

Boy: "Yes sir."

In the crow's nest, the lookout looks.

"I'll be damned. Somebody has taken the bloody binoculars."

| 2010 |

# The Hangman's Handbook

Written after the hanging of
Saddam Hussein, December 2006

In view of the recent hanging, a summary of The Hangman's
Handbook may be of interest.

1. A course in hanging, concluding with a Certificate in
Hanging, is the preferable route for the hangman. The stan-
dard course includes elements of physics and physiology,
such as the distance that the prisoner must fall after the trap
door is opened and the effect of the sudden arrest of the fall
on the prisoner's neck, nervous system, and blood pressure.
Weight of prisoner correlated with distance of fall must be
accurately calculated. A well-fed prisoner is the hangman's
best friend.

2. An alternative to certification is apprenticeship. Much
can be learned from observation. Often apprenticeship runs
in families, just as acting, plumbing, or politics do.

3. Improvisation is the least recommended path for a
hangman. The chance for error and embarrassment increase
exponentially with lack of practice.

4. As for the choice between breaking the neck and as-
phyxiation, informed hangmen will choose the former for

its neatness and speed. The professional consensus is that lynchings here at home were carried out by non-specialists, since they lacked both neatness and speed.

5. The masks for prisoner, hangman, and assistants are traditionally black, but they can come in assorted colors if the participants so wish.

6. Taunting the prisoner is unacceptable. The best course is to allow the prisoner to choose the topic of conversation.

7. The official videotape of the hanging should not be supplemented with an unofficial videotape. This practice can lead to confusion about what actually happened.

8. It is desirable to finish the trial before the hanging.

9. The president or prime minister should order a cost/benefit analysis of the hanging before it occurs, weighing the possibility of its precipitating a civil war.

10. The word *hangman* in this summary can be construed as singular or plural, male or female.

| 2007 |

# Everybody's Political ABCs

**A** is for animals, which we all are.

**B** is for beasts, which some of us are.

**C** is for catastrophes, which statesmen usually guess wrong about when trying to avoid them.

**D** is for the public be damned, if you are not part of the public.

**E** is for enemy. When convenient, they are called friend.

**F** is for future, when you will be well-off, happy, and healthy.

**G** is for God, who is on our side. Unless you are on the other side, in which case God is still on your side.

**H** is for hysteria, the emotional state in boardrooms when social legislation is mentioned.

**I** is for I, the author, an optimist.

**J** is for jeering at people who don't agree with us.

**K** is for killing, necessary to save the world from more killing.

**L** is for Love Thy Neighbor as Thyself, which does not apply to non-neighbors.

**M** must be for money. You count if you have it. You don't count if you don't. M is also for mythology, which says that you count either way.

**N** is for nation, each of which is superior to all others.

**O** Oh! Surprise when something turns out well.

**P** is for poor, a state to be avoided at all costs except by those who can't.

**Q** is the question for which there is an answer. Very few people know it at present.

**R** is for religion, in which there is a well-established division between theory and practice.

**S** Sympathy for others. Usually followed by punishment.

**T** is for timidity. An attitude toward rules made by somebody else.

**U** is for understanding disasters, a mental faculty used after they occur.

**V** is for virtue, so precious that we store it up to be used sometime in the future.

**W** is for war, always started because the other side is about to start it.

**X** is for xenophobia. Fear and hatred of outsiders because they fear and hate us.

**Y** You. How do you fit into the scheme of things?

**Z** Zzz. You won't understand any of this until you wake up.

| 2006 |

# Five Variations on Jack and Jill

## Variation One: In the Style of Isaac Bashevis Singer

I was walking down Krchmalnik Street when I saw Jill carrying a bucket. "I must go home and work on my novel," I thought. But my feet had other ideas and they hastened their pace until Jill and I were walking side by side.

"Oy, Jack. Why are you here? Why are you not in your apartment writing?"

"Why are we in Warsaw? Why is Hitler on one side and Stalin on the other? Does God care where I am or where you are? Let him make a miracle and put us somewhere else."

"Oy, Jack. Don't talk that way. Miracles happened in the old days. They don't happen now."

"Give me your bucket," I said. "I'll help you fetch a pail of water."

As we walked up the hill, I felt myself drawn to Jill. I had known her since childhood. She never grew up. And yet I wanted her. How could this be? I already loved Hanka and Basha. Must I also love Jill? Why not? It sometimes happens in fiction that a man loves several women at the same time, but it always happens to me. A demon preys on my nerves until I am compelled to submit to its demands. Maybe several demons, one for each woman.

"Jill, I'll lower the bucket and get the water."

She leaned close to me to watch. I dropped the bucket down the well and put my arms around her.

"Oy, Jack. This is not permitted."

"It's permitted, Jill. It's permitted. When a man loves a woman, everything is permitted."

"Oy, Jack, I've never been touched by a man. My body is shivering. I must go home. Mother is waiting."

I couldn't let go. She struggled. We fell and rolled all the way down the hill. We were covered with dirt from head to foot. And the bucket was at the bottom of the well. Jill started to cry. "Mother will be angry."

"Don't worry. We'll tell her thieves attacked us."

"No, Jack, That would be a lie."

"It's better to lie than to upset your mother."

Jill's tears stopped and she laughed. "You look funny, Jack."

| 1981 |

## Variation Two: In the Style of Franz Kafka

Jack woke up one morning and found that he had been transformed into a giant insect. He had trouble getting off his back but managed to slip off the bed sideways, thinking that he had drunk too much schnapps the night before and was hallucinating. As he looked in a mirror at his spindly legs, beady eyes, and elongated beak, he realized that he had really changed into a horrible-looking bug.

His mother knocked on the bedroom door to remind him to get up for work. He replied in a strange voice that he was ill. Then his sister Jill knocked. Getting no answer, she opened the door and let out a scream when she saw the giant insect. "Where are you, Jack? What is this horrible bug doing in your room?"

"It's me, Jill. Something terrible has happened."

Before Jill could reply, their father walked into the room and was repelled by what he saw. "I knew you would come to no good." He stormed out.

Then an assistant manager from the office came to inquire why Jack was late after five years of perfect attendance.

"So. You are wearing a masquerade costume at nine in the morning. You have besmirched a perfect record. Don't bother to come back to work," he snarled as he slammed the door behind him.

"What can I possibly do for you?" Jill wondered out loud. "Maybe I should call a doctor."

"I'm terribly thirsty," Jack said to Jill, in his strange voice.

Jill replied, "Climb down from the ceiling, Jack, and let us go up the hill to fetch a pail of water."

Jack covered himself with a sheet and walked up the hill with Jill.

"Perhaps you're right. I have a terrible headache. I should see a doctor," said Jack.

Just then, Jack fell down and broke his crown and Jill came tumbling after.

At the bottom of the hill, Jill found that Jack had died.

His family was torn between sorrow and relief. They decided on a memorial service with a closed casket.

| 2011 |

## Variation Three: In the Style of Ernest Hemingway

The enemy had advanced to the top of a hill and their fire raked the entire valley. Jack was a medic who had been wounded in a previous engagement while driving an ambulance. Now his entire detachment was scattered. As an officer he ordered a fleeing soldier to help get the wounded out of the ambulance into the safety of the woods. The soldier kept running. Jack unholstered his pistol and shot the runaway dead.

Jack and his fellow medic Jill had just enough time to run into the woods to take cover as an advancing column of men rounded a corner in the road.

"We're cooked," said Jack. "Our entire battalion is cooked."

"I know it," said Jill.

Jack took a flask of whiskey out of his pouch, and after giving Jill a swig, drank down the entire contents.

"You're drunk, Jack," said Jill.

"I know it," said Jack. "And I'm terribly thirsty."

"There's a stream that passes by further up the hill," said Jill. "I've seen local peasants going up there with buckets. We've got to get up there somehow."

"I'll take a pail from the ambulance and sneak up there in the dead of night."

"You can't go up by yourself," said Jill. "Not the way you're wounded. I'll go up."

"Too dangerous. I have a gun. You don't. We'll have to try to go up together."

They moved farther into the woods and up the hill. They came to a clearing where remnants of their unit had gathered. Several cocky young military policemen were swearing at three elderly officers.

"You abandoned your troops!"

One officer replied, "They scattered before enemy fire. We could do nothing."

The MPs scoffed and ordered the three elderly officers to be taken into the woods and shot.

"Let's get out of here," Jack said to Jill. "If we stay, we're cooked."

They fled until they came to the stream further up the mountain. Jill dipped the pail into the stream and filled it. Jack and Jill drank their fill. Then Jack took another flask of whiskey from his pouch, and after Jill had a swig, Jack finished it off. Jack grabbed Jill and Jill grabbed Jack and they fell down upon the ground and tumbled under the trees until the light of dawn.

| 2011 |

# Variation Four: In the Style of George Bernard Shaw

*A well-furnished flat in a London suburb not far from a hill with a well at the top. Two comfortable chairs angled toward each other are occupied by Jack and Jill.*

JACK. Let's go up the hill to fetch a pail of water.

JILL. First of all, we don't need any water. Second of all, I'm perfectly able to fetch a pail of water without your help.

JACK. I was just using the idea of fetching a pail of water as an excuse to spend some time with you.

JILL. Then you should say what you mean and mean what you say.

JACK. I confess that I'm a bit shy in using a direct approach.

JILL. I'm not shy at all. I don't want to spend any time with you.

JACK. [*Hearing thunder.*] I just heard thunder. It's about to rain. Do stay out of the rain and have a cup of tea with me.

JILL. I am not made of sugar. I will not melt in the rain. But I will have a cup of tea with you.

JACK. [*Rings for maid.*] Jane, some tea and scones, please.

JANE. Yes, Mr. Jack. Right away. [*The doorbell rings.*]

JACK. Excuse me. Let me see who that is. [*Opens the door.*] Mother! How nice of you to drop by. Let me introduce you to Jill.

MOTHER. How do you do?

JILL. How do you do?

JACK. [*Rings for Jane.*] Another cup of tea for Mother.

JANE: Yes, Mr. Jack.

MOTHER. I've come to give you an important bit of news. The Prime Minister has asked me to join the cabinet as Home Secretary.

JACK AND JILL. [*Together.*] Congratulations!

MOTHER. Jack, I shall need you in drawing up an agenda for the Prime Minister. He so enjoyed your last novel. I'm sure he will be delighted to have you present in drawing up the agenda.

JACK. With pleasure, Mother. But are you not aware that Jill won the Man Booker prize last year for her novel, *Do Not Listen to Your Heart*?

MOTHER. Oh Jill, how fine of you to win the Man Booker prize. Please do join us in drawing up the agenda for the Prime Minister.

JILL. I will do so. But only on one condition. Jack must go up the hill with me to fetch a pail of water.

MOTHER. Be a good boy, Jack, and go up the hill to fetch a pail of water with Jill.

JACK. Well, Mother, if I must. [*The doorbell rings. Jack opens the door.*] If it isn't the Prime Minister! Do come in, sir.

MOTHER. So good of you to come by, Mr. Prime Minister. I have lined up two of the best writers in all England to help draw up the agenda for the Home Secretary meeting.

PRIME MINISTER. Ah, yes. The author of *Do Not Listen*

*to Your Heart* and the author of *Pig Tales.* Jill, why does your heroine, Claire Voyant, finally listen to her heart?

JILL. She had to go through all the stages of not listening to her heart. Too much of an intellectual. But the life force finally got her.

PRIME MINISTER. And Jack, why do you call ordinary people pigs?

JACK. Because they are too inclined to listen to extraordinary people. They should think for themselves. [*The bell rings.*] Mrs. Prime Minister. Welcome.

MRS. PRIME MINISTER. [*Oblivious of others.*] Thank you, Jack. I cannot stay. I have come for the Prime Minister. You are late for dinner. Come home at once. Do not keep the Queen waiting.

PRIME MINISTER. Yes, dear. Coming at once. [*They leave.*]

MOTHER. I must also be toddling along. Bye Jack dear. Bye Jill. [*Mother leaves.*]

JILL. Let's go up the hill and fetch a pail of water.

JACK. We don't need water.

JILL. I know we don't need water. I need you. I have tested you and you have passed the test.

JACK. What is the test?

JILL. You have powerful friends. Perhaps they will make you powerful. Then you can be an equal partner with me. Almost equal. Women by nature are stronger than men. [*They exit. Jane enters with a tray of tea and scones.*]

JANE. Where has everyone gone? What fickle people! What snobs! I shall give notice to Mr. Jack when he returns. His friend the Earl of Sandwich has proposed and I have accepted. [*She puts down the tray and tidies the room. Jill returns.*]

JILL. [*To Jane.*] Jack fell down and broke his crown. He will be writing his memo in hospital. Meanwhile I shall head over to 10 Downing Street since I have been invited to dinner with the Queen.

| 2011 |

## Variation Five: In the Style of Jane Austen

Father was quite exasperated with Mother. As he sat in his study, Jill entered. He looked up from his book as Jill spoke.

"Mother insists that I meet the gentleman who leased Netherfield Park. I have no taste for it. I shall meet him in due time at the next ball."

"Mother will not be at peace until you and your sisters are safely married. I suppose I shall go meet the new neighbor and invite him to tea."

"Oh Father, please do not go out of your way."

"I shall go out of my way, or I shall have no end of scolding by Mother."

The new neighbor proved to be a kindly young gentleman, and quite rich. But clearly he preferred Jill's older sister. Before anything was said and done, he returned to London.

Quite by surprise, the kindly young gentleman reappeared with a friend, Sir Jack, who proved to be quite the opposite of his companion, aloof, stiff, and condescending, as Jill was to find out.

Sir Jack was so taken with the rural charm of Hertfordshire, that he let Pemberley Estate, known far and wide for its magnificent views of the countryside.

The first encounter at the annual ball was quite unpleasant. The kindly neighbor introduced Jill to Sir Jack, who immediately turned his back and walked away. I cannot abide him, Jill thought. He is haughty, self-absorbed, and rude.

In spite of his hauteur, Sir Jack had taken a liking to Jill. Within a month, he returned to London with his friend. His absence was nothing to Jill until she met Sir Jack's younger sister, who spoke of her brother's exceptional kindness to her and all his friends. How puzzling, thought Jill.

During the following month, Jill's aunt and uncle invited her and a small group of friends to inspect the great halls of several nearby estates, including Pemberley, with its magnificent paintings and objects of art. Sir Jack being away, Jill saw no harm in going along. As the group was admiring a gallery of paintings at Pemberley, Sir Jack unexpectedly returned.

The unexpected appearance of Sir Jack proved quite disturbing to Jill, whose face reddened in confusion and anger. At the same time, Sir Jack acknowledged to himself his admiration for Jill.

"Allow me to show you the magnificent view from the top of the hill," he said to Jill. "Perhaps we can go up the hill together to fetch a pail of water at the well."

"You have been rude to me, sir. I shall not go up the hill with you and I shall not fetch a pail of water."

"I beg your pardon. I did not intend to be rude. I am thought by strangers to be aloof. But my friends know better. I am often preoccupied with matters of business, which makes me appear aloof to those who do not know me. Kindly allow me to prove to you that I meant no offense."

These appeasing words softened Jill, who accompanied

Sir Jack to the top of the hill to observe the magnificent vista and fetch a pail of water.

Sir Jack almost fell down, and surely would have broken his crown as he stumbled on a stone, but Jill caught him in her arms and arrested his fall.

The next day, Father wryly said to Mother, with a bit of suppressed mirth in his tone, "I have heard that Jill is going to be married."

"To whom?" asked Mother in alarm.

"To Sir Jack," answered Father.

"Oh heavens," cried Mother. "How glorious. How glorious," as she smothered Father with kisses.

| 2011 |

## Eternal Bliss

"Madam, I was flirting with Alfredo the butler, when he slumped to the floor."

"And?"

"He is dead — with an erection."

"Dead with an — ?"

"Yes, dead with an — "

"Then he is dead with an — "

"He will need a coffin with a — bump?"

"Yes, he will need a coffin with a — bump. Unless we — "

"Oh, no madam. That would be such a cruel indignity."

"Such a cruel indignity."

"He cannot go to heaven without a — "

"No. He cannot go to heaven without a — "

"We must allow him to enjoy eternal bliss."

"Yes. We must allow him to enjoy — "

"Poor man."

| 2006 |

# I Divorce Myself

I received a letter from the Social Security Administration addressed to Myron E. Sharpe. A reference was made in the body of the letter to "your spouse, Myron E. Sharpe." I had not remembered marrying myself. But the advantages were obvious, such as agreeing on when to take a walk, when to have lunch, when to reread *War and Peace*, and so forth. But the problem of bigamy started to bother me. Could I be sent to Guantanamo for questioning? I walked around myself three times, saying, "I thee divorce; I thee divorce; I thee divorce." I also took the precaution of going to a lawyer to have my marriage to myself annulled on the grounds of incompatibility, which, of course, was a stretch.

| 2006 |

# Grand Old Times

I remember from my childhood how the veterans of the North and South came together once a year to reminisce about the war.

Their ranks grew thinner year by year, nostalgia grew greater, until none were left to meet.

We felt a pang for these old men, tenderly coming together, sixty, seventy years after they raged with blood-filled eyes.

Now, no longer a child, I wonder the outcome if young men tenderly came together with foresight, not blood-filled eyes.

| 2005 |

# On Books

Francis Bacon wrote the best essay on books, so the most I can hope for is second best. Bacon wrote: "Some books are to be tasted, some books are to be studied, some are to be swallowed whole." He failed to say that most books are not to be read at all because they are worthless. That leaves about .0005 percent of all books in print that should be tasted, studied, or swallowed whole.

Bacon did not discuss newspapers or magazines, the great obstacles to reading books. They are easier to read. They arrive periodically. They tempt us to get them out of the way before we concentrate more intensely on books. I once was like the boy who passed an apple orchard. The farmer said he could eat all he wanted. He started with the leaves. By the time he ate them, he had no room for apples. In those days, I subscribed to 6 newspapers and 21 magazines, being intent on keeping up to the minute on everything.

After several years, I found that the same stories repeated 27 times told me very little that I didn't already know, so I canceled everything but one newspaper and two magazines. Even then the repetition day after day was stultifying and I found that reading the headline or the title was usually sufficient to know what the writer had to say.

That leaves the question of what to read. As a student, you must read books that deal with the fundamentals of the subjects you are studying. As a specialist, you must read the advanced books in your field. All the while, you are instructed by English teachers to read whatever is fashionable among novels, plays, essays, and poetry.

When I was young, I read books beyond my grasp and puzzled to make out their meaning as a child puzzles to make out the meaning of words. I remember reading a book putting Shakespeare down as a victim of echolalia only to be corrected by Shaw's *The Sanity of Art*. A time comes, or ought to, when judgment allows a distinction between sense and nonsense.

After having gone through all this, if your desire to read has not been preempted by movies or television, you can read haphazardly or according to a plan. You can estimate how many books you can read by making some calculations. I saw an article with calculations, but forget what they were and am starting fresh. Suppose you can read two books a week. In a year you can read 104 books. In ten years you can read 1,040 books. Say you live to 90 and start this plan at 30. You then have 60 years to read, or 6,240 books. If you read haphazardly, you will chance to read some great books. If you plan to read only great books, you may become surfeited and leave off before 90. So you must incorporate some second- and third-rate books in your plan. Then you must still decide which ones to taste, swallow whole, or read with care.

That is a matter of preference and interest that will

change as you go along. You may put highly rated books on your list and find them tedious and discard them. You may put lengthy books on your list and find that they consume more time than you are willing to give. I have been reading *Middlemarch* for 20 years and still intend to finish it. But other books, like *Remembrance of Lost Time*, may be lost to me forever. In four attempts over 30 years, I have never been able to get past the first 100 pages. A list, by the way, is not necessarily a written list. A list may simply be many books you have in mind that you intend to read.

An overlooked aspect of books for book readers is their mere presence. Nothing is more satisfying to a book reader than walking past his or her bookshelves, glancing at a title, and remembering all the associations of ideas, feelings, people, and places aroused by a mere glance. It is as good as reading the book over again. That is why I recommend never lending a book. A lent book is rarely returned and you have penalized yourself far beyond the dollar value of the book. Keep friendships intact by buying your friend a new copy.

What is the purpose of reading books? Great literature is usually represented as a humanizing influence. This cannot be true if the main social currents are dehumanizing. Many of Hitler's henchmen read Goethe and Schiller and loved their dogs, but Goethe and Schiller did not make them better people. Neither did their dogs. Books are part of the numerous influences on people and if other influences make them decent, books will help them understand more readily and more deeply how to be decent.

Finally, there is the matter of what is in books. If you have the compulsion to know everything, as I do, you must read, read, read. Then do and do, do, do, and do the best you can.

| 2006 |

*Since writing this, I have finished* Middlemarch *and intend to try reading* Remembrance of Lost Time *again.*

# A Surprise for the Dictator

> On October 1, 2011, the *New York Times* reported that
> an increasing number of Russians were taking up
> permanent residence abroad.

Once upon a time, a dictator won an overwhelming victory at the polls. Leaders of the opposition party had been put in jail for subversion. The people realized that the country was stagnating under the duly elected dictator. Corruption prevailed. Citizens started to take long vacations abroad. They started to take up permanent residence in foreign countries. The home country began to suffer from brain drain. Then it began to suffer from brawn drain.

One morning the dictator woke up and rang for his assistant. Nobody appeared. He put on his robe, opened the bedroom door, and looked around for somebody to blame. He went upstairs and downstairs, into the parlor, the dining room, the kitchen, the conference room, the exercise room, and the underground bunker. The building was empty.

He went out on the balcony and looked around. The square was empty. He got on the phone and called the prime minister. The prime minister did not answer. He turned on the TV and the screen was blank.

The dictator got dressed and hurried down to the carport. The drivers were gone. He got into a limousine and drove around the city. It was deserted. The shops were closed. The bars were closed. The banks were closed. The police were gone. No one could be seen anywhere.

He called the president of the United States and learned that everybody in his country had emigrated.

Everyone lived happily ever after. Except the dictator.

| 2011 |

# The Man of Many Masks

The president noticed that he had started to lose control of his facial expressions. He called in a leading neurologist, who ran a series of tests and then explained that the facial nerves controlled by the brain were losing their conductive power. The process usually occurred as a result of some trauma. The president replied that running for president was trauma enough, given that he had to say anything that any particular audience wanted to hear.

The president soon realized that he could not appear in public with a blank expression. Having seen all kinds of masks in movies, he got in touch with an ingenious Hollywood mask-maker.

After describing his condition, the president said, "I need to appear engaged in public, in different ways with different audiences. In each case, I need to appear natural."

"The art of mask-making," replied the mask-maker, "has become so sophisticated that my team can make you masks suitable for any occasion that you desire."

Within a short time, the president learned the proper way to put on a mask. He then appeared in public with the appropriate expression for each occasion. Among bankers, he looked bankerly. Among workers, he looked workerly. Among generals, he looked like the commander-in-chief.

Among foreign leaders, he looked like a leader. At military funerals, he looked solemn.

Within a few months, the president began to lose his sense of engagement with the audiences he was speaking to. He called in a leading psychiatrist who explained that his emotions had been numbed by the need to appear to be all things to all people. "The result of this syndrome" explained the leading psychiatrist, "is a total confusion about what you stand for."

After contemplating this disconcerting predicament for several days, the president concluded that he stood for one solid, immutable cause. He stood for himself.

The next morning, as he was putting on a mask in front of his mirror, he was horrified at what he saw.

| 2011 |

*Poetry*

# The Day the World Came to an End

I

How then did Eve feel
when she learned
that her son had killed her son?
Did she moan and wish that God had never created her?

And Adam.
Did he shed manly tears?

Are you Cain?
Are you Abel?
Are you Eve?
Are you Adam?

I hear moaning in the air.
Maybe it is the wind.
I feel tears in the sky.
Maybe it is the rain.

II

On the way home passing through Tallil
men smoking, drinking
on stoops

women washing clothes
stepping over bodies
before sunset
sand in me
sweat on me

Suddenly three young boys
their backs to the sun
step before the Humvee
an AK-49 in the hands of one
with thirty rounds
he slowly turns it toward me
my safety is off
*Why don't they run?*
I press the trigger

They lie shredded in the street
Silence
I see the bolt is gone
I see the stock is gone
I see the trigger is gone
The gun run over in the street

I'm back in New York now
Moonlight comes in my window
I see blood on the floor
I hear a car horn blare
I jump out of bed

I get my gun

I yell

   Stop that goddamn noise

Or I'll kill you

III

Death comes randomly

It's your turn to come with me, soldier

It's your turn to come with me, Iraqi

Soldier at the checkpoint

Worshipper in the mosque

Mother in the market

Baby in the cradle

I am the soldier

I am the Iraqi

I am at the checkpoint

I am in the mosque

I am in the cradle

Today I pushed the button that released the bomb

Today I died in the house hit by the bomb

Today I beat prisoners at Abu Ghraib

Today I was beaten at Abu Ghraib

Today I jumped from the Tower

Today I saw bodies falling from the Tower

I kill myself. I am a terrorist
I am killed. I am the victim of a terrorist

I kill myself on a cross
I resurrect myself
The stigmata remain on my hands and feet
forever

I betray myself
I judge myself
I search for myself

The mosques are burning
The arsonist burned them

There are no monuments
For those kicked by a boot

IV

I am a Jew
I am a Christian
I am a Muslim

Shoved into boxcars
shot in the stomach
my family parted
to the gas chambers
unless you are strong

then you work.
Into the crematory for being unlucky

Muslims, Christians, Jews
Hide in basements
In sewers
In attics
Behind walls

Until the basements crumble
The sewers overflow
The attics burn
The walls collapse
Until the world comes to an end.

Do you hear the Scream?
It sounds like this

**AAAAAAAAAAAAAAAAAAAAAAAAAAAAAAAAAAAAA**

V

The Terrorist-in-Chief is well satisfied.
The Murderer-in-Chief smiles his crooked smile
in conspiracies of the ignorant with the ruthless.

Air filled with the Scream.
Arms raised to heaven
the hands stretched out
asking God *Why?*

The Scream volume is turned up by deaf men.

So easy for the aggrieved to follow and shout

"Kill them!"

So hard to say at last

**"Stop!   Stop!   Stop!"**

VI

I am not one who feels nothing for others

I am not one who believes lies

I do not hide under a rock like an insect with secrets

You and I

are united in death—

or united in life

Where do you stand?

Do you Scream silently or aloud?

I know where you stand.

VII

I hear moaning in the air.

Maybe it is the wind.

I feel tears in the sky.

Maybe it is the rain.

## Notes

1. The incident at Tallil (part II) is described by John Crawford in his book *The Last True Story I'll Ever Tell* (2005). The phrase in italics, "Why don't they run?" is a quote from the book, page 217. The sequel in New York is entirely fictitious.

2. The phrase "conspiracies of the ignorant with the ruthless" (part V) is from "Tendril," a poem by Adrienne Rich that appears in *The School Among the Ruins* (2004), page 106.

| 2006 |

# Letters to Emily Dickinson

Dear Emily Dickinson,

Wherever you are.

You asked a question —

In a letter —

To an eminent person,

Wanting to know —

If your poetry lives.

He never gave —

An affirmative answer —

Equivocating.

Missing the obvious.

Your poetry lives —

Be assured —

In posterity.

Inebriate of air

Are we — who have glimpsed —

Sublimity.

It's true — our mind is larger —

Than the Universe.

Yet the Universe is larger — than we.

But let me mention — one advantage —

When seen in the proper Light.

The Universe — can't write.

If matter and energy cannot be created or destroyed

We shall be here forever

In one form or another.

So don't worry —

About the future.

It's guaranteed.

We will have one.

We were always here, too.

In the past, I mean.

I hope you feel better now.

If we are reassembled

at some future date

God forbid

We should suffer —

Amnesia.

Emily Dickinson

Was a recluse.

For the World

She had no use.

But in her Mind

She did embrace

The entire Human Race —

And things Beyond —

That have no name.

We know — with certainty —

It was not in vain.

Non cogito, ergo non sum.

A great loss, to be sure.

But one — we won't notice.

What is poetry?

I am not averse — to a lilting verse.

There's always time — for a melodious rhyme.

Meter we savor — never out of favor.

Feet? Good to repeat.

Does it scan — according to a plan?

Alliteration — all fascination!

But what is poetry?

The *revelation* — if there be one.

My mind contains the universe — or it would

if I understood what the universe was.

Physicists now tell us the universe is numerous —

A wheel of Swiss cheese with globes bubbling up

each a universe itself. I accept

the universes, of course, but still don't know

how the Big Cheese — got there. Does it

go on forever in time and space,

or does it occupy a limited place?

Why Swiss cheese instead of — nothing?

By and by we'll understand,

computer in hand, as we eat away

At this puzzling array of palpable — something.

Emily Dickinson!

The questions you asked

Are still unanswered.

We've reason to think

Of cosmic betrayal.

Yet doubters persist

In suggesting this:

Betrayal of self —

Then deadly denial.

We act insanely —

Mocking the few

Who act humanely.

Your soul will settle

When we confess —

The thorn's in us —

Not in — Him.

We thrust ourselves against a barrier

Like a bee on a windowpane.

The bee will die in another try.

So think of this, oh gentle reader —

You're not a bee — so cogitate —

And ruminate — on where you're bound —

And take the route the long way round.

Fame is a bee.

It has a song —

It has a sting —

Ah, too, it has a wing.


    Emily Dickinson

Life is a bee.

It has a song —

It has a sting —

Ah, too, it has a wing.


    Variation

Poems in the attic

Found post-mortem.

Emily Dickinson

Began to live

When she died.

# Testimony of a War Criminal

The genocide in the Balkans was followed by war
crimes trials. I wrote the following reflections about
a low-ranking Serb in 1997 based on an article in the
*New York Times*.

I'm nobody, so why am I here?

A pipefitter is nobody important.

Don't blame me for being unemployed

at the time of my arrest.

I didn't want a war,

but nobody asked my advice.


It's true I killed a woman,

then went into an alley

and puked.

Her blood ran freely

leaving a stain on the ground.


Then killing was easy,

just a routine job.

I killed fifty,

maybe sixty —

I wasn't keeping count.


I feel no pity

and neither do they.

They killed, raped, and tortured
my innocent people
in wild bursts of fury
over countless years.
I can't feel sorry,
no more than a surgeon
who lives with blood and pain
for a highly honored cause.

Hate eats my stomach.
But I hate even more
the men who started the war.
I did this for nothing.
I could have been killed
for a few empty promises:
just a better job,
just a bigger house.
The generals and the politicians—
they got the bigger houses,
they got the better jobs.
I got nothing—
but betrayal.

I stand before my family,
my wife and my children,
with rage in my heart.
Don't blame me

for what took place.

I'm nobody.

They've got—

the wrong man.

| 1997 |

# The Good Soldier

After Nazim Hikmet

He calls me

He promises me

He deceives me

He asks me to die


I come

I believe

I am deceived

I die


| 2005 |

# Iraq – Free at Last

Inspired by remarks of Secretary of Defense Donald
Rumsfeld after the fall of Iraq, April 2003, who added,
"Stuff happens."

There's no telling what a free people will do

They loot museums

They kill one another

They torture prisoners

They follow the mullahs

They rule over women

They give oil to the rich

They murder their liberators

A free people can do most anything they want to

| 2005 |

# Spread It All Around

Soldiers, dear
It is your fate
To set up a clerical state

Women, dear
Shariah rules
Submit, don't be fools

Mullahs, dear
The oil will flow
When you say so

President, dear
You must take pride
Spreading freedom far and wide

| 2005 |

# Give It to Them

In honor of, and in memory of, the poet Omar Shapli
after the publication of *Them*, 2007.

Give it to Them.

Take it from Them.

Knock them on the head

until they're all dead.


They keep coming back.

I can't keep track.

Who are they?

It's hard to say.


And a ratatat. Brave of you

to think of that.

| 2007 |

# Connecting Flights

In honor of the poet Lou Barrett, whose collection, *Connecting Flights*, I had the privilege of publishing in 2006.

All the birds flock together

Every one in flight

In the blue vault of light

Oh that we could flock together

Understanding each other

Like the birds in flight

| 2005 |

# Lessons from New Orleans

Don't be poor.

Don't be old.

Don't be sick.

Don't be black.

Don't live in New Orleans.

| 2005 |

# Quote from an Unidentified Source in Washington

I do not like thee, Doctor Fell;

The reason why I cannot tell.

But this I know, and know full well,

I do not like thee, Doctor Fell!

For all I care, you can go to hell!


(If a prosecutor asks me to talk,

Well, I'm afraid I will have to balk.)


| 2005 |

# I'll Never See Him Again

Cindy Sheehan's son Casey was a U.S. soldier
killed in Iraq on a mission in Sadr City on April 4, 2004.
The following is an excerpt from a statement Sheehan
made outside the George W. Bush ranch in Crawford,
Texas, on August 17, 2005, rendered in poetic form.

I'll never see him again.

I'll never get to hear his voice again.

I'll never get to hug him or kiss him or joyfully welcome my

grandchildren.

This is about flesh and blood.

This is what we're here for.

# You Lied to Us

In a TV ad on August 23, 2005, Cindy Sheehan
summarized her indictment of the president.
I have put this excerpt in poetic form.

You were wrong about the weapons of mass destruction.

You were wrong about the link between Iraq and Al Qaeda.

You lied to us

and because of your lies, my son died.

# My First Son

These are the words of Marie Fatayi-Williams
in Tavistock Square, London, after her son
was killed on a bus in the bombings of July 7, 2005.
I have put these excerpts from the *New York Times*
of July 17, 2005, into poetic form.

It's time to stop and think.

We cannot live in fear because we are surrounded by
hatred.

Look around us today.

Anthony is a Nigerian, born in London, worked in London,
he is a world citizen.

Here today we have Christians, Muslims, Jews, Sikhs,
Hindus

all of us united in love for Anthony.

Hatred begets only hatred. It is time to stop this vicious
cycle of killing.

We must all stand together, for our common humanity.

I need to know what happened to my Anthony.

He's the love of my life.

My first son, my first son, 26.

He tells me one day: "Mummy, I don't want to die, I don't
want to die. I want to live. I want to take care of you. I will
do great things for you, I will look after you, you will see
what I will achieve for you. I will make you happy."

And he was making me happy. I am proud of him.

I am still very proud of him but I need to know where he is.

I need to know what happened to him.

I grieve, I am sad, I am distraught, I am destroyed.

| 2005 |

# Selected Poems from
*Thou Shalt Not Kill Unless Otherwise Instructed,* 2005

# Heartbreak House

We have books.
We read The New York Times.
We watch CNN.
What can we do?

We talk at the table.
We invite friends.
We express dismay.
What can we do?

We have difficulty eating.
We have difficulty sleeping.
We have difficulty getting through the day.
What can we do?

We will not go along.
We are sorry for those who will.
We talk incessantly.
What can we do?

# I Saw This

I lived on the edge of holocausts and wars.

By mere chance I was spared from pestilence and
starvation.

I came near but not within the grasp of dictators and
torturers.

The poor lived around me but not too close.

For no particular reason I was spared the wretchedness of
prison.

I had work when others were consumed by despair.

I had rooms and a garden while others suffered
humiliation.

I read the news of massacres at breakfast in a comfortable
chair.

The good people took little pleasures between catastrophes.

They took little pleasures during catastrophes that
happened somewhere else.

Leaders were the most innocent of all.

They knew no other way.

I never thought it had to be this way.

I always believed there was another way.

I merely report what I saw.

# The Eyeball

Their heads were targets sticking above the armor.
Their Humvee armor was home-made junk.
They were blasted by shrapnel from C-4 explosives.
Ten marines had their brains blown out.
They jumped to the road and began to return fire.
They jumped to the road and began to return fire.

Then the marines were blasted by grenades.
Arms and legs lay scattered on the road.
Heads and torsos as well as an eye.
The captain ordered the eye to observe
and see where the fire was coming from.
He ordered a finger attached to a trigger
to pull the trigger and return the fire.
To pull the trigger and return the fire.

But the eye was turned in the wrong direction.
He ordered the hand to turn around the eye.
But the hand was too dazed to follow his orders.
The captain directed the leg to kick the hand.
The hand came to and turned around the eye.
The hand came to and turned around the eye.
The captain asked, where the hell shall we shoot?
The eye looked at the target and the finger pulled the
trigger.

Soon the finger was blown to bits
and the fighting had to come to a halt.
The medics arrived and swept up the pieces
and sent them to Walter Reed Medical Center.
And sent them to Walter Reed Medical Center.
Some of the arms and legs and heads
were too far gone to make the trip.
They were gently dropped into body bags.
They were gently dropped into body bags.

But the eye survived. Its name was Frank.
The eye was depressed and the eye was angry.
What kind of life could he have as an eye?
But then his eyelid turned up at the hospital
and was grafted back onto his eye.

All trauma patients under the nurse in charge
rage in the ward in desperate anger.
The arms and legs and the hands and heads
rage in the ward in desperate anger
trying to put their lives back together.
Trying to put their lives back together.
What kind of life can we live
as arms and legs and hands and heads?
We aren't ourselves anymore.

Then Stella came into the ward,
another eye that was scraped off the road.
Frank and Stella looked eye to eye.
Frank and Stella became friends and lovers.

They spoke to each other in an unknown code.
They spoke to each other in an unknown code.
Then they were married in the Walter Reed chapel.

Frank the Eye monitored in a bank.
Jorge the Arm turned nuts on bolts.
Sam the Leg got a job as a bouncer.
Bill the Head watched out for terrorists.
Lucille the Torso worked as a model.
Bruno the Hand worked sorting diamonds.

But Stella was unhappy, she wanted a child.
By a stroke of good fortune the medics had found
the sperm and eggs of Frank and Stella
the sperm and eggs of Frank and Stella
spilled on the highway outside of Ramadi.
They vacuumed them up and put them on ice
and sent them to Walter Reed Medical Center.
They were put in a dish and there were united.
A surrogate was found to carry the child.

Who says wars don't have happy endings?
But the captain was kicked out of the Marines.
He let his men down in their time of need.

They were put in a dish and there united.
Who says wars don't have happy endings?

# The Wrong House

I meet with other mothers. My son is a marine. I'm against the war. But I'm for my son. I meet with other mothers whose sons are marines. We don't talk about politics. We talk about our sons.

I watch TV at three in the morning for names, I'm too unquiet to sleep. I search the web for news, not about who is fighting, but about who was killed.

I ask on the phone, how are you, do you need anything, did you get the package, but I don't ask where are you and what are you doing, and he doesn't tell me because he doesn't want me to know and I don't want to know.

I hear the DoD announce a name and I think, thank God he wasn't mine, and then I reproach myself.

The war has been over several times, and we are freeing twenty-five million people several times, and we don't talk about it.

We all fear two marines coming down the front walk, it's an image that we avoid, but we can't avoid it.

The day came, I saw two marines coming down the front walk, my back was turned, I saw them reflected in the mirror.

They're coming to the wrong house! I'm sure they're coming to the wrong house! I'm sure they're coming to the wrong house!

My hand is on his coffin, my head is on his coffin, the earth is on his coffin, hands reach out to me, hands touch me, hands comfort me, but they cannot reach me, they cannot touch me, they cannot comfort me.

Thank you, thank you. Your hands cannot reach me. They cannot touch me. They cannot comfort me. It is of little use. It is of little use. I rewind time. It is of little use. I am on a far shore alone. I am on a far shore alone.

# His Heart Was Heavy

Christ slipped back into town.
His heart was heavy with what he saw.
His heart was heavy with what he heard.

Christ felt that irreparable damage had been done.
His heart was heavy with what he saw.
His heart was heavy with what he heard.

Christ heard a great sigh and a great moan.
His heart was heavy with what he saw.
His heart was heavy with what he heard.

Christ perceived a burden he could not lift.
His heart was heavy with what he saw.
His heart was heavy with what he heard.

Christ heard a mob approaching.
Christ saw a mob approaching.
And the mob took him roughly.
And the mob took him as a man condemned.

And they crucified him.
And they crucified him.
He never said a mumbling word.
He never said a mumbling word.
He just bowed down his head and died.
He just bowed down his head and died.

# The Life of a Snowflake

I looked out the window
and saw a thousand snowflakes falling
dazzling in their ephemeral existence

One snowflake mused
I'll probably live a normal span
a few moments
but is there life after melting

The snowflake god replied
your constituent parts will join the earth
and so transformed
you'll live forever

## Intelligent Design

The children remain unenlightened.
Doesn't that leave you frightened?

The teachers' teaching is phony.
The kids suspect it's baloney.

The nose was designed for glasses.
They teach you that in the classes.

The backside was designed for sitting.
It also serves for shitting.

You must keep your breast under cover
Never to be touched by a lover.

The penis on the statue is missing.
The church forgot about pissing.

The Big Guy thinks it's vain
Ever to use your brain.

It's so decided by the Sages.
Don't mess with the Middle Ages.

# The Helpless Giant

He celebrates himself.

He invites his soul.

Men and women are as good as he is and are at his side.

He sings and dances among them and children join in and
are not afraid.

He and they possess the earth and the skies.

He luxuriates on the grass. In the evening there is a great
heat

in the fire and he and they warm themselves before it.

He climbs mountains with ease and swims rivers with ease.

He strides across continents with ease.

He cultivates farms, builds cities, and shouts a great shout
around the globe.

He lifts up the poor and the sick and gives a home to
teeming masses.

He walks with free men and free women and former slaves
who are now as free.

He reads books and recites poems and with his hands
makes marvelous devices.

He goes to war in the company of men, he is present in the company of women who do the work at home, he defeats a savage enemy and then he and they rebuild war-torn lands.

Time passes and he goes into the jungle, deeper into the jungle, into the darkness.

His feet are caught in tangled vines and his right arm is caught in tangled vines and the stench of the jungle sickens him. He swings with his free hand and savagely kills, rabbits, lions, deer.
Vines tangle him and snakes mar his body and the venom sickens him.
Wild birds gall and bloody his face.
His feet sink into marshes and they engulf him.
He spends his power. He cannot move. He cannot move in and he cannot move out. He bears blindness and pain and scorn.

Once he reached the clouds and wore robes of gold and silk and doffed them for homespun cloth when at his ease.
Once men and women came around to sing and dance and children came near and now they are afraid.
Once he possessed the earth and skies and luxuriated on the grass and celebrated himself. No longer.
He does not climb mountains nor swim rivers nor shout a lusty shout.

He does not wear robes of gold and silk and commune with men and women and come near children.

He cannot take his ease unless the darkness lifts and sight returns to his eyes.

He cannot take his ease unless the swoon passes and he remembers himself and recognizes himself and accepts himself and celebrates himself and invites his soul once again.

# Selected Poems from
## *A Requiem for New Orleans,*
2006

---

# Where Are You, God?

I am poor and black
abandoned
abandoned all my life.

I am poor and white
abandoned
abandoned all my life.

Where are you, God?
Where is my salvation?

I wonder if they that mourn are blessed:
I wonder if they shall be comforted.

I wonder if the meek are blessed:
I wonder if they shall inherit the earth.

I wonder if, when men revile me,
and persecute me, and say all manner
of evil against me, I am blessed.

I wonder if I ask, it shall be given me.
I wonder if I seek, I shall find.
I wonder if I knock, it shall be opened to me.

*Dies irae, dies illa,*

*Quantus tremor est futurus,*

*Quando judex est venturus*

*cuncta stricte discussurus!*


This day, this day of wrath,

What trembling there shall be,

When the judge shall come

To weigh everything strictly!


Where are you, God?

Where are you?

You say you are merciful, but I have not received mercy.

You say you are just, but I have not received justice.

You say the door is open, but I have not been allowed to come in.

Creator, what have you created?

Where are you?


You are not my shepherd;

I am in want.

You do not allow me to lie down in green pastures;

You do not restore my soul.

Yea, I walk through the valley of the shadow of death.

I fear evil: for thou art not with me.

*I am the Lord thy God. Do not despair in the darkness.*

*I am all that you have dreamed.*

*Look around.*

*Look, Man and Woman, to the earth as well as heaven.*

*Man, Woman, what have you created?*

*You who have tilled the land.*

*You who have built cities.*

*You who have become cunning.*

*You who have lifted up the mighty though he be a grain of sand among ten thousand.*

*I gave you the earth, you who are ten thousand many times over.*

*Look around you.*

*Look within you.*

*Look and see what you have dreamed.*

*You who have become cunning.*

*You who have lifted up the mighty though he be a grain of sand among ten thousand.*

*Look around you.*

*Look within you.*

*Look and see what you have dreamed.*

*Man, Woman, abandon not yourselves.*

*Listen not to honeyed words.*

*What have you created from what I have created?*

Hear my answer, O God.

I who was perplexed and deceived.

My reproach is idle.

I judge and reproach myself.

Nor am I a grain of sand blown in the wind.

I who was ignorant will help my neighbor and say:

Do not despair in the darkness.

Look and see what we have dreamed.

We will rebuild the levees.

We will rebuild the houses.

We will beautify the city with heart-chords of music and
sway-rhythms of dance.

We will awaken from a deep sleep

And look into ourselves

And remember what we have dreamed.

We will awaken from a deep sleep

And remember what we have dreamed.

# A Dream Deferred

What happens to a dream deferred?
Does it fester, does it dry up, does it stink?

Does it yank you back?

What happens to a dream deferred?
The waters come rushing in.

Will the waters cleanse America's name?
Or will America stay just the same?

# Selected Agitations from *Challenge*

# Little Red Riding Hood

Ms. Hood was fourteen when the incident occurred. It was to leave its mark on her psyche. Her psyche had already been badly scarred by that eccentric name. It made her brash and flamboyant. People have been known to change their entire personalities as a result of changing their shoe styles. When Ms. Hood changed her name to Rebecca, it calmed her down considerably. But that happened later.

It must be admitted that Mother was a big part of the problem. Mother was forty and the single head of a household. These facts depressed her. Living in Scarsdale depressed her. Working for the Fed depressed her. Grandmother's recent retirement to a house in the woods depressed her.

"Poor Grandmother, poor Grandmother. All alone in the woods." These words were addressed to no one in particular, but Ms. Hood chose to reply.

"Grandmother weighed the costs and benefits and opted for early retirement. She elected to take the lump-sum payout under her pension plan to make a down payment on a house. As for living in the woods, if you can call New Canaan the woods, there has been a marked population shift to the exurbs for at least a decade. Grandmother is following the trend."

Mother sighed. "Poor Grandmother, poor Grandmother. Alone in New Canaan." "I'll take Grandmother a picnic basket if it will make you feel better," offered Ms. Hood.

"Alas, we haven't got a picnic basket since we never go on picnics," sighed Mother. But at length a picnic lunch was placed in a brown paper bag. "Don't talk to strangers. Don't hitchhike." These were Mother's parting words.

Being brash and flamboyant, Ms. Hood did talk to strangers and did hitchhike. She was picked up by a character with singularly large ears, eyes, and teeth. He drove a 1974 Mercedes 250.

"What's your name?" he asked.

"Little Red Riding Hood. What's yours?"

"The Wolf," replied The Wolf.

They had a good laugh over that.

"Where to?" asked The Wolf.

"I'm taking this brown paper bag with a picnic lunch to my Grandmother's house deep in the woods of New Canaan. Grandmother had a high marginal propensity to save during her working life. She doesn't need picnic lunches in brown paper bags. But Mother is in a reactive depression and experiencing anhedonia. I'm doing this for her."

"Mother a bit sour, eh? But Grandmother is right as roast duck. Well, I'll drive you as far as I'm going. You can easily walk the rest of the way."

They had a good laugh over that, too.

The Wolf was in his mid-forties and hungry. He was one of those wolves who always has the things that money can buy without ever having any money. But life was passing him by.

"Can I take advantage of this girl's credulity?" he thought to himself as he stopped the car. The girl turned to him and asked, "Is this where I get out?"

"Yes," was his sardonic reply.

They laughed again.

The Wolf drove directly to Grandmother's house and knocked on the door. Grandmother was eating muffins and "Who's there?" sounded like two blasts on a muted trombone. Grandmother's forceful voice could not be stilled even by muffins.

"The Wolf," said The Wolf.

"Come in," said Grandmother, "and have some muffins. It's lonely in these woods, even if it is New Canaan, and I wouldn't mind having somebody to eat my muffins with. Mind you don't take more than your fair share."

"You are uncommonly kind," said The Wolf, wolfing down a muffin.

"Don't put me on," said Grandmother, eating another muffin.

"I must insist that you are uncommonly kind," replied The Wolf, wolfing down another muffin and breaking into tears all at once.

"Cripes, don't carry on. I can't stand maudlin scenes. Take a tissue."

The Wolf took a tissue and blew his nose. "Muffins always make me maudlin," he sobbed. "I once had a cafe that served muffins. It was taken over by creditors. That is why muffins always make me maudlin. When I meet someone who is generous, the shock of it and the cafe and the muffins bring tears to my eyes. I could eat you, you are so uncommonly kind," he added.

"You'd better stick to the muffins," remarked Grandmother.

Some time later, Little Red Riding Hood arrived at Grandmother's house after a long walk through the woods. Not hearing anyone stirring, she lifted the latch and walked in. There in Grandmother's bed she saw The Wolf. "My, what big eyes, ears, and teeth you have," was the first thought that ran through her mind. As The Wolf was thinking, "The better to—" Little Red Riding Hood cried out: "The Wolf has eaten Grandmother!"

A passing woodsman heard the cry and dashed into the house. He took a shot at The Wolf and missed. "Cripes," shouted Grandmother, poking her head out of the covers. "You've put a hole in my Chippendale headboard. Not since I retired as curator of the Detroit Museum of Paleontology have I met such a numskull. You meddlesome booby, you gawking blockhead, you interloping dunce, you fossilized herringbone, you—"

Just then, Mother, who had felt guilty about sending Little Red Riding Hood when she should have gone herself, drove into Grandmother's driveway. Hearing the shouting, she ran into Grandmother's bedroom.

"Grandmother, what are you doing?" asked Mother.

"Cripes, can't you see I'm eating muffins with The Wolf? Can't a body eat muffins in peace? Here, have some muffins. You have some too, Little Red Riding Hood. And you, you numskull," said Grandmother, alluding to the woodsman, "you might as well have some too."

At this, Mother looked at the woodsman. The woodsman looked at Mother. They felt involuntarily, irresistibly attracted to each other as they ate their muffins.

Little Red Riding Hood took it all in. "Mother said not to talk to strangers and not to hitch a ride," she thought. "Yet, if I hadn't disobeyed Mother, I would not have met The Wolf. If I had not met The Wolf, he would not have come here to eat muffins with Grandmother. If he had not come here to eat muffins with Grandmother, I would not have cried out. If I had not cried out, the woodsman would not have come in. If the woodsman had not come in, he and Mother would not have felt involuntarily, irresistibly attracted to each other as they ate their muffins. Life is uncertain and there are few rules that apply to all cases. By breaking the rule in this case, things turned out well. But probably this case should not be considered a precedent. It is hard to know when to obey Mother and when not to. One never has enough information to be sure."

Grandmother and The Wolf got married and bought a Burger King franchise, ending a long string of failures for The Wolf. Mother and the woodsman also got married, ending Mother's reactive depression. Little Red Riding Hood changed her name to Rebecca and bought stylish shoes. They all lived happily ever after.

| September 1977 |

# The Truman Show

When I was about five years old, I entertained the fantasy that my mother, father, aunts, uncles, and acquaintances were actors who performed their parts in my presence and then reverted to their natural non-acting selves when they were out of sight. Unfortunately, I never found out if I was right or wrong.

I was not surprised to discover that a movie was made out of the likes of my childhood angst. In this comedy of exquisite sadism, written by Andrew Niccol, Truman Burbank is adopted at birth by a giant television company — novel, but of doubtful legality — and everyone around him is an actor: his mother, father, best friend, wife, coworkers at a spurious insurance agency that sells spurious insurance to spurious individuals, shopkeepers, street-sweepers, etc., etc., etc. This whole monstrous fabrication is paid for by corporate advertising. To drive the artificiality of this conceit into the heads of the most obtuse, all the actors overact: the mother is oh too-too motherly; the best friend is so awfully true blue; the wife is ever so wifely; and the father, well, he drowns early in the story and returns later as a derelict: there has to be some concession to reality. As to his not-to-be college sweetheart we'll come back to her later. I must retract what I said about the obtuse. The effect was designed for the obtuse and observant alike.

Everyone who watches *The Truman Show* on television—and it is the most popular show in the history of shows—knows that Truman's whole life is a fake. Only Truman himself is not a fake. But he is hoodwinked, bamboozled, and hornswoggled about living in a world created by someone else.

That person is Christof, ironically named, a master of deception who directs the show from a control room in a huge dome that covers the pristine town of Seahaven, built on an island inside the largest television set in the world. Even the sun, moon, stars, clouds, and sky are fake, more dazzlingly real than real, all composed of painted scenery and light show put on within the dome. [If I remember correctly, a half-moon is shown fifteen to twenty degrees away from the setting sun, an optical impossibility.] Five thousand cameras allow the audience to see Truman twenty-four hours a day.

The premise of *The Truman Show*—the portrayal of duplicity—is realized by the clever merging of illusion and reality as well as illusion within illusion. Everything that we see has several meanings. We see events—fiction to begin with—but we know the events are telling several stories simultaneously, one perceived by Truman, one perceived by the staff of the studio, one perceived by the spectators watching television in the movie, and one perceived by us sitting in the theater. We are flooded with perceptual dissonance, which stoops or rises to get our attention; it's hard to say which. We see actors acting as actors [Shakespeare, Pirandello], actors acting as non-actors [ditto], and actors acting as directors [also ditto]. The real spectators [you and I] are set up for an evening of loathing. The screenwriter has found a perfect metaphor for manipulation.

No sham, however elaborate, can be without flaws. Truman begins to notice them when he is about thirty. A spotlight falls out of the sky onto the street a few yards from Truman with the curious label "Serius." As he drives to work, an actor-newscaster attempts to cover up the mishap by announcing that debris has fallen from a plane. [The set is bigger than any of us imagined.]

Truman's car radio jams and, with characteristic American ingenuity, he kicks it several times and hears that he, Truman, is turning a corner: he has accidentally tuned in a radio frequency directed to the actors.

He notices that several people circle the block repeatedly in the same sequence. His "wife" Meryl brushes off this observation as the result of an overactive imagination.

He conceives a desire to go to Fiji, as far away from Seahaven as it is possible to get. Meryl suggests that they conceive a baby instead: what actresses will do for a living these days is truly remarkable.

As the affable Truman becomes more and more suspicious, he loudly claps his hands in a supermarket as a test. Nobody looks up; Christof has evidently failed to coach his actors in spontaneity.

Now while they are driving he confides in Meryl that he is the center of some kind of gigantic conspiracy and they must get off the island immediately. But, since every word of his is heard in the control center, a traffic jam suddenly materializes on previously empty streets and he can't move his car.

It's not as though Truman wasn't warned about the conspiracy. One member of the cast and only one cannot stomach the fraud. Lauren, his not-to-be sweetheart in college, blurted out the truth one night on the beach, but she was hustled off the set by her actor-"father," who hastily explained that Lauren was a little mental and was given to blurting out nonsense on a regular basis. Subsequently, the camera intermittently cuts to Lauren, now Sylvia — her real name — sitting in her room somewhere in America watching *The Truman Show* in a state of righteous indignation. Strategically placed behind her for us to see if we look carefully is a poster announcing a Free Truman Rally. A few people out there are not just spectators after all.

Jim Carrey shows us that a really serious actor was hiding behind the exaggerated facial contortions of his previous roles. He makes the transition from insouciant insurance salesman to terrified fugitive with honor to his not always distinguished profession. Laura Linney is an effective complement as his excessively smiling and reassuring actress-nurse "wife." One of her most incongruous scenes shows her pitching a commercial for cocoa to a television camera with her broad faux smile while she is at the same time offering to make Truman a cup of the same cocoa; he stands incredulous at her artificiality. Ed Harris—Christof—plays an impenetrably self-confident executive whose words and demeanor make the case for a leader who is ruthless for the good of others.

Later we see Truman, leafing through his wedding album, notice with consternation that Meryl's fingers are crossed in a photograph of their postnuptial embrace. Even the wedding was a fraud.

Of course Truman has to escape. In alarm at the thought of the longest-running and most-watched TV show coming to an abrupt halt, Christof cues the sun in the middle of the night—a startling sight even in a movie—and sees Truman sailing away toward the horizon. The horizon, you recall, is the inside of a dome. But I have said enough. All of which I assume you will have forgotten when you see the movie, if you haven't already.

*The Truman Show* is a treacherous metaphor for America in the last quarter of the twentieth century that somehow managed to make its way out of Hollywood and say something true and significant. We are living *The Truman Show*. We are passive spectators watching Truman—millions of Trumans who are in a predicament—and we have lost the knack of doing anything about it. A small number of us are Christof, manipulating Truman and everyone else, buying the acquiescence of politicians who are strangely silent about the plight of Truman. Some of us are Meryl and the other actors and crew who have talked themselves into thinking that

Truman doesn't need help. A few of us are running corporations that sponsor the program that torments Truman. A minority of us are Sylvia, who organizes rallies to protest the treatment of Truman to no avail.

Christof himself announces: "We accept the reality of the world with which we're presented; it's as simple as that." (I owe this quote to Janet Maslin of the *New York Times*, who must have brought a penlight so that she could take notes.)

The quote is quite right up to a point. Truman is trapped in his culture and we are trapped in ours. And yet a movie like *The Truman Show* could not have been made in the 1930s or 1940s, when millions of us or our parents or grandparents were active participants instead of spectators, even if we or they only pulled the lever for Roosevelt or bought War Bonds. No one would have thought of making a movie showing spectators sitting at home doing nothing about hardships that affected three-quarters of the country. Sometimes we don't accept reality; we do something about it.

Perhaps Truman escapes all by himself without help from any of us in the end. It only happens that way in the movies.

| September 1998 |

# JKG Versus the Angel

## A Puppet Play

*JKG lies asleep in his bed, snoring. An angel descends into the room.*

ANGEL [*Female.*] Wake up, JKG. I've been sent to talk to you. [*Shakes him.*] Wake up.

JKG. [*Rubbing his eyes.*] Just say the word. I'm ready.

ANGEL. Ready for what?

JKG. To do another TV series.

ANGEL. If you'd look, you'd see I'm not a TV producer.

JKG. [*Sitting up and looking.*] Oh, Angelina. It's you again. Every time I write a book, you come to question me.

ANGEL. There's nothing wrong in writing a book. There's nothing wrong in doing a TV series. But the way you do it! You—

JKG. —commit the sin of pride. Don't scold. I know what you're going to say. But consider the facts.

ANGEL. I have considered the facts. The facts are that an economist is offered thirteen hours of prime time. He has a rare opportunity to sing the praises of his profession. But he just says a few words about Smith, Marx, Keynes, maybe one or two others, and nothing about Sismondi, Petty, Locke, Mill, Jevons, Menger, Wieser, Walras—

JKG. —which would bore people to tears. Please—

ANGEL. Please nothing. You refuse to talk about them because you prefer to talk about yourself.

JKG. [*Rises and strokes the angel's wings.*] Do calm yourself, Angelina, and let me call for some tea. [*Rings.*] You angels must try to see things in proper perspective. Almost everything that needs to be said can be said by discussing Smith, Marx, and Keynes. Smith is like Aeneas, founder of the Roman dynasty. There were those who came before and those who came after. But when you have told the story of Aeneas' travels from Troy to Italy, you have told all, especially if you tell it from the vantage of a later century as Virgil did. Aeneas was the center of a mythology; so is Smith. Those who believe myths don't regard them as myths. They are all the more powerful for that. If you look at economics as mythology, you will see that I was right to stick to Smith.

ANGEL. What about Marx?

JKG. A kind of countermyth. Like Goethe's Mephistopheles. He derides all that was previously thought sacred. Today we live under the myths of Smith and Marx, they share the world. Could I have done better than to use my thirteen hours to explain how things really are without the myths?

ANGEL. This is what I mean by pride, JKG. [*A knock at the door.*]

JKG. The tea has arrived. Come in.

*Smith enters with tea followed by Marx with cake.*

SMITH. Some devil shoved this tray into my hands as I came up.

MARX. *Irgend ein Teufel hat mir dieses Tablett Kuchen zu tragen gegeben.*

JKG. The myths have arrived. With tea and cake.

MARX. Do not be impertinent to your elders and betters. I founded the science of society and Smith laid the groundwork.

JKG. Forgive the joke. I always joke when startled. Great as you are, your claims are exaggerated. Let a thing happen; you have explained it. Let the opposite happen; you have explained that, too. Any explanation that appears valid regardless of what happens is no explanation. It is metaphysics. The theory of value is an example. It cannot be falsified by facts. Here's the best I can say for you. You made a reasonably honest but mainly unsuccessful attempt to get away from grand philosophical systems toward a science of society. That was a great accomplishment—for your time.

SMITH. Poppycock. It's perfectly clear that society breaks down if things are not done my way.

MARX. Worse than that. It's perfectly clear that society breaks down if things are not done *my* way.

JKG. The world is divided between you. That's why we're all going to the devil.

*Mephistopheles enters through the open door.*

MEPHISTO. I heard you mention my name. I should have come long ago. I'm a great admirer of yours.

JKG. Thank you. Words fail me.

MEPHISTO. Not at all. Do consider me a friend. As Faust did.

JKG. Oh, Faust. A humorless fellow. Something of a rat, too. I couldn't have been cruel to Gretchen for all the world. I would have made her happy. Faust was a bumbler with women. I'm not.

MEPHISTO. It was Gretchen who was a bumbler with Faust. But opinions differ in these matters.

JKG. Surely you didn't come to discuss Gretchen.

MEPHISTO. No. Of course not. I've come to discuss your book. I'm a compulsive reader, you know. Read everything of yours including *Indian Painting*. Now what I want to know is: when does the science of society really begin?

JKG. When we clear away the myths. There are bits and pieces of science in Smith and Marx. But science is just beginning. It really began with Keynes if you want a name. He didn't attempt a whole system; just a few relationships.

*Enter Keynes.*

KEYNES. I don't know who I am.

JKG. [*Rushing to him.*] But you are Keynes. I recognized you at once. [*Enter Keynes Number Two.*] Good heavens!

KEYNES #2. My identity is not at all clear.

JKG. One of you is an impostor!

*Enter Keynes Number Three.*

KEYNES #3. Not at all. Not at all.

KEYNES #1. I am Aggregate Demand Keynes.

KEYNES #2. I am Financial Instability Keynes.

KEYNES #3. I am Cost-push Keynes.

KEYNES #1. Three in one.

KEYNES #2. One in three.

KEYNES #3. But terribly confused.

MEPHISTO. Come now, fellows. That's the result of not writing clearly. You must face it like a man—like men—like whatever the devil you are.

MARX. [*Stentorian.*] I demand to be heard. This queer triplet should not be welcome here. They are apologists for the status quo.

MEPHISTO. We are all apologists for one thing or another. No one is free of bias. The remedy for that is skepticism. Follow my example.

KEYNES #1. True. No one is free of—

KEYNES #2. —bias. The remedy for that is—

KEYNES #3. —to leave the bias out when you are doing science.

SMITH. No one is free of bias. The remedy for that is to know your bias. But I would rather call it commitment to an ideal.

JKG. All of you are right.

ANGEL. Straining for a paradox. Typical. It's enough to make an angel weep.

JKG. No, my dear Angelina. I am not straining. Take the law of diminishing returns. No matter what the bias of the person who believes it, it's a true statement, free of bias. Then take the theory of laissez faire. No matter how many true statements free of bias it may contain, the person who believes it sees the world with a bias or a commitment to an ideal, as Smith says. Finally, take both of the above. A person can be skeptical about whether the first applies to a particular situation and about whether the second is a valid means to reach the stated ideal. We must have bias, be free of bias, and be skeptical of bias all at once. Three in one. One in three.

SMITH, MARX, KEYNES NUMBERS 1, 2, AND 3 [*together*]. Paradox! Paradox! Paradox! Paradox! [*They run around the room in a circle. Smith and Marx hurl their trays at JKG.*]

JKG. Get lost. You are apparitions from the past and cannot judge the present.

*He picks up a cake knife from the floor and slices off their heads.*

SMITH. Milton Friedman will hear of this!

MARX. I'm going where I'm wanted. To Paul Sweezy's house!

KEYNES 1, 2, AND 3. I must really try to get my heads on straight. [*Calling.*] Joan Robinson! Joan Robinson!

*They leave with their heads tucked under their arms.*

ANGEL. What a mess. Broken crockery and cake all over the room. [*Angelina, Mephisto, and JKG take brooms and sweep.*]

JKG. Most of my life I have been sweeping up the debris of the past.

MEPHISTO. You speak like a disciple of mine. Economics is rubbish from the past.

JKG. Do not misunderstand me. In my books and on

television, I discuss the giant corporation, its symbiosis with government, the poor countries, the arms race. The present realities. These are the main subjects of economics today — or more accurately, of political economy today. If you go to Washington, London, Paris, Bonn, or Rome with theories from the past which conflict with realities of the present, you will be committing a sophisticated kind of fraud. It's not out of egotism that I gave my own views — not entirely any-way — but because no other view fits. No other view except for those of a few friends — they will know who they are.

ANGEL. Look here, old pal. You've made a pretty good case for yourself. But you fail to mention that you advocate socialism. You don't think that you can slip that through in a torrent of words when everybody's yawning and ready to go to bed, do you?

JKG. There is no acceptable rationale for the power that resides in the great corporation. Management is autono-mous — uncontrolled by market forces, by government, by employees. It's a thoroughly undemocratic arrangement and I have only suggested that the present boards of directors be dismissed and new ones be made up entirely of public mem-bers, responsible to carry out public policy without interfer-ing in details of management. My hope is that public policy can eventually be made to correspond to public interest.

MEPHISTO. Quite so. I myself am a socialist. Whenever I find myself in agreement with the majority, I hasten to re-examine my views. Why? Because the majority allows itself to be persuaded by the powerful, and the powerful are interested in finding justifications for their power.

JKG. When we have socialism, I presume the majority will have the power.

MEPHISTO. Then you will belong to me. [*Takes his hand and pulls.*]

ANGEL. No, to me. [*Takes his other hand and pulls.*]

MEPHISTO. You cannot serve God until you have served me. Self-interest first.

ANGEL. You cannot serve the devil if you want to serve me. Altruism first. [*Both pull harder.*]

JKG. I have much experience. Life is both giving and receiving. I have done my share of both. Smith be damned. Marx be damned. So stop pulling.

MEPHISTO. But tell us which one you will go with.

JKG. I didn't know I had a choice.

MEPHISTO. Heaven and hell are a matter of preference. People get whichever one they want.

JKG. I will keep that in mind. Meantime my preference is to go back to bed. But first I will kiss Angelina. [*Which he does. Mephisto goes through the floor with a bang and a puff of smoke. Angelina flaps her wings and floats through the ceiling in radiant light and to the accompaniment of heavenly music.*]

| May 1977 |

# The Poorest Rich Country in the World: Address to the Graduating Class of 2011

Distinguished president, provost, and faculty; parents and graduating class of 2011:

You have taken the risk of inviting me as your commencement speaker knowing that my views on everything are negative. But no harm will come to your alma mater, Beneficent College, because tomorrow the college will close its doors permanently.

The endowment is broke, the state is broke, and Washington is broke. Gather all your grades, letters of recommendation, and yearbooks by the end of the day because nobody will be here tomorrow to give them to you. Get your own subscriptions to *Challenge*. The library will be closed.

The college cannot be harmed. You will be harmed. You will be harmed for inviting a radical speaker, and this fact will be in your records for the rest of your lives and thereafter. Your diminishing chances of employment will be diminished further by your rash decision.

Here are my negative thoughts for the class of 2011.

I looked at your course requirements. I am sure most of you have read *The Iron Heel*, *Brave New World*, *1984*, *Fahrenheit 451*, or *Player Piano*, and recognize a dystopia when you see one. These books depict a world in which everything becomes worse in the future, and here we are in the future.

In these books, monopoly trusts rule the country. Nobody knows the truth anymore except the ruling class. We are perpetually at war. All knowledge of history and society is obliterated except among a few protestors. Work is done by machines and the unemployed are left to scramble for themselves.

Well, Jack London, Aldous Huxley, George Orwell, Ray Bradbury, and Kurt Vonnegut were waving red flags to warn us about a possible future. Here we are in the future. We used to be the richest rich country in the world. Now we are the poorest rich country in the world. We have become Dystopia USA.

You have been taught that we have all kinds of information. But have you been taught that most people don't know the meaning of the information? We have all kinds of information about the universe, but we don't know the meaning of the information except for those who make guesses. And they don't know the meaning either. We have all kinds of information about the USA, but we don't know the meaning of the information, except that teachers are the cause of our problems. A good guess. Or immigrants. Another good guess.

The ones who control the political marketing of ideas control the guessing. That's why the teachers are to blame. Never mind that they pay more taxes than GE, the largest corporation in the world until proven otherwise, which pays none. True, immigrants don't carry a great tax burden, for which they are to blame.

Students, you know that political marketing takes money and organization. You know that unions used to be the type of organization that did most of the political marketing for the public. Back in those days, we were less of a dystopia than we are now. The unions have been beaten. Their political marketing is sad.

Did you know that free speech, press, and assembly are harmless formalities exercised freely, and tolerated because they have no effect on policy? Contrary to the predictions made in all the literary dystopias, the leaders of our system don't need to establish a dictatorship. They already have one. Freedom of speech, press, and assembly create the illusion that we have no such thing as a dictatorship. I'm guessing that people prefer to hold on to their illusions.

So here's my advice, graduating class of 2011. Have fun, go to the beach, go dancing, listen to music, read books, make love, and when you know more, help to make the USA less a dystopia and more a country where everybody has enough to eat and drink, a nice place to live, a good education, a well-paying job, and equality for men, women, blacks, Latinos, gays, and American Indians. Where the army, navy, and air force are shrunk to a manageable size, and where teachers are not blamed for everything that is wrong. Or immigrants.

Just a reminder. Don't forget to collect your possessions after the diplomas are distributed.

| May 2011 |

Photo by Liz Sharpe

## *About the Author*

Mike Sharpe is the founder of M.E. Sharpe, Inc., which publishes academic books and journals in the social sciences, international studies, business, and management information systems. His previous books include *John Kenneth Galbraith and the Lower Economics; Thou Shalt Not Kill Unless Otherwise Instructed: Poems and Stories; Requiem for New Orleans*, a collection of poems; and *America in Decline*, collected articles from *Challenge* magazine.

For Product Safety Concerns and Information please contact our EU
representative GPSR@taylorandfrancis.com
Taylor & Francis Verlag GmbH, Kaufingerstraße 24, 80331 München, Germany

www.ingramcontent.com/pod-product-compliance
Ingram Content Group UK Ltd.
Pitfield, Milton Keynes, MK11 3LW, UK
UKHW021608240425
457818UK00018B/447